All About Disneyland: A Kid's Guide to the Happiest Place on Earth

Educational Books For Kids, Volume 42

Shah Rukh

Published by Shah Rukh, 2024.

ALL ABOUT DISNEYLAND: A KID'S GUIDE TO THE HAPPIEST PLACE ON EARTH

First edition. October 30, 2024.

ISBN: 979-8227448163

Written by Shah Rukh.

Table of Contents

Prologue

Welcome, future Disneyland adventurers! Are you ready to discover the happiest place on earth? This guidebook is made just for you—kids who are curious, excited, and ready to explore all the magic Disneyland has to offer!

Whether it's your very first visit or you're already a Disneyland pro, there's always something new and amazing to discover. From thrilling rides that twist, turn, and splash, to friendly Disney characters ready to give you a high-five, Disneyland is like stepping into your favorite storybook. In these pages, we'll uncover secrets that even grown-ups might not know, explore different lands with their own special stories, and give you tips to make your visit unforgettable.

Each chapter will take you on a new adventure—from the wild rides in Tomorrowland to the delicious churros waiting on Main Street, and even tips on meeting Mickey, Minnie, and the gang! Disneyland is packed with mysteries, fun facts, and even a few hidden surprises that only the best explorers know how to find.

So, grab your mouse ears, bring along your excitement, and let's jump into the magic. This is your guide to having the best day ever at Disneyland—because here, your dreams really can come true!

Chapter 1: Welcome to the Magic Kingdom

Welcome to the Magic Kingdom, the most enchanting place at Disneyland! Imagine stepping into a land where every dream can come true, and magic seems to sparkle in the air. From the moment you pass through the entrance gates, it feels like you're entering a whole new world. The Magic Kingdom is filled with castles, characters, and adventures waiting around every corner. There's something incredible to see or experience wherever you look, from the towering castle at the center to the smiling faces of people who work there, ready to make your day special. The Magic Kingdom isn't just one place; it's like a group of magical lands all gathered in one park. Each land has its own theme, unique look, and story, so it feels like you're journeying to different worlds without ever having to leave. It's a place where everyone feels like they can be a kid, no matter how old they are, and there's an adventure for everyone.

As soon as you enter, you're greeted by Main Street, U.S.A., a charming little street that looks like it's from long ago, with colorful buildings, sweet-smelling bakeries, and cheerful music playing. It's like taking a step back in time, with horse-drawn carriages, an old-fashioned cinema, and even a trolley that you can ride! You might catch a glimpse of Mickey Mouse himself or other beloved characters strolling around, ready to meet you for a picture or sign your autograph book. At the end of Main Street stands the magnificent Sleeping Beauty Castle, a shimmering sight that's especially beautiful when it's lit up at night. This castle is the heart of Disneyland, and walking through it feels like stepping into a fairytale.

Once you're through the castle, you have so many choices! Maybe you'll explore Adventureland, where jungle mysteries and treasures await. Here, you'll find rides like the Jungle Cruise, which takes you on a wild river adventure with funny guides who share jokes along the way. You might also come across Indiana Jones, the famous explorer, and hop on a thrilling ride that twists, turns, and takes you through ancient ruins and traps. Adventureland feels exciting and full of wonder, and you never know what's around the next corner.

In Fantasyland, you'll discover where the fairytales live. This is where you'll find classic rides like Peter Pan's Flight, where you get to soar above the rooftops of London on a magical ship. There's also Dumbo the Flying Elephant, where you can control your own flying elephant and take in views of the whole park. In Fantasyland, it feels like anything is possible, and you can visit all the classic characters from stories you know and love, like Snow White, Alice in Wonderland, and Pinocchio. It's like stepping into the pages of a storybook and meeting these famous characters right where they live.

For brave adventurers, Tomorrowland might be the next stop. This land is all about the future and exploring space! With attractions like Space Mountain, a thrilling roller coaster in the dark, it feels like you're zipping through stars and galaxies. There's also Buzz Lightyear Astro Blasters, where you team up with Buzz Lightyear to save the galaxy from the evil Emperor Zurg by blasting targets as you spin and turn. In Tomorrowland, there's so much to do, and it's full of robots, aliens, and inventions that make you feel like you're living in a futuristic world.

If you're into the Wild West, Frontierland is the perfect place to visit. This land is set up like a real frontier town from the past, complete with a riverboat, old-time saloons, and a gold-mining mountain called Big Thunder Mountain Railroad. Here, you can hop on a thrilling runaway mine train and zip through caves and canyons. Frontierland feels like a whole different time and place, and it's a spot where you can let your inner cowboy or cowgirl run wild.

And then there's New Orleans Square, a place full of jazz music, spooky stories, and delicious food. This part of Disneyland feels like a little slice of New Orleans, with its fancy buildings, winding streets, and jazz music drifting through the air. Here, you'll find the Haunted Mansion, a spooky (but fun!) ride through a ghostly house filled with silly and mysterious spirits. There's also the Pirates of the Caribbean, where you get to take a boat ride through pirate battles, towns, and treasure chests. In New Orleans Square, you'll feel like you're on a grand adventure through history, with a little spookiness and excitement mixed in.

Critter Country is another fun area where you can find friendly forest creatures and splashy fun. One of the most popular rides here is Splash Mountain, where you join Br'er Rabbit on a log-flume adventure that ends with a big splash! Critter Country has a cozy, woodsy feel, and it's filled with gentle rivers, shady trees, and characters from stories like The Many Adventures of Winnie the Pooh.

Throughout the Magic Kingdom, there are parades with colorful floats, music, and characters that dance and wave to everyone. You might even catch a fireworks show at night, where the sky lights up in amazing colors, and it feels like the whole park is celebrating. These parades and shows make you feel like you're part of a grand celebration, with everyone cheering and singing along.

And of course, there's delicious food everywhere you go! From giant turkey legs and churros to Mickey-shaped ice creams and pretzels, there's a treat for every taste. Each land has unique foods, so you can try different things as you explore.

The Magic Kingdom at Disneyland is truly a place where every moment is filled with wonder, excitement, and fun, and each visit feels like a new adventure waiting to happen. With so much to see, discover, and enjoy, it's a place that feels like home to Disney fans and makes everyone feel like they're part of something magical. No matter what you love, there's a corner of the Magic Kingdom that's perfect for you, filled with fun, friends, and memories you'll never forget.

Chapter 2: The Story of How Disneyland Began

The story of how Disneyland began is a tale as magical as the park itself. It all started with a man named Walt Disney, who was known for creating some of the world's most beloved cartoon characters like Mickey Mouse, Donald Duck, and Goofy. Walt was a dreamer who believed in creating happiness, and his imagination knew no limits. He thought of ideas and stories that no one else had dared to bring to life, and people all over the world adored his cartoons and movies. But Walt didn't want to just make movies—he wanted to build a place where families could have fun together, where kids and adults alike could laugh, play, and escape from their everyday lives. He dreamed of a place where magic was real, where the characters he had created could come to life in a way that felt real to everyone who visited.

Walt's idea for Disneyland came from many different places, and one of them was his time spent with his daughters. He loved taking his daughters, Diane and Sharon, to parks and places where they could ride carousels, eat popcorn, and just have fun. But Walt often found himself wishing for a park that could offer even more—a place with clean streets, friendly faces, and, most of all, places where parents and kids could enjoy rides together. In the 1940s, he visited a few amusement parks around the country, but they didn't have what he was looking for. Most amusement parks back then were a bit rundown, crowded, and sometimes not very family-friendly. Walt began to imagine something completely different, a park that would feel like stepping into a magical world where everything was possible. He knew he wanted it to be different from any other amusement park in the world.

The dream began to take shape when Walt shared his ideas with a few close friends and colleagues. At first, people thought he was dreaming too big. They doubted that such a grand idea could ever come to life. But Walt was determined, and he never gave up on his vision. He spent years planning, sketching, and perfecting every detail of what would later become Disneyland. He even used his own money to start funding the park, selling his vacation home and borrowing money to make sure the dream could happen. By 1953, Walt and his team, which he called "Imagineers" (a combination of "imagination" and "engineers"), were working day and night to create the blueprints and designs for this magical place. Walt chose a plot of land in Anaheim, California, a town that wasn't well-known at the time, but Walt had big plans for it.

Building Disneyland was no small task. The land was a big, empty field filled with orange groves and dirt. They had to completely transform it, building roads, setting up electricity, planting trees, and creating a layout for each part of the park. Every corner of Disneyland was carefully planned. Walt wanted each land to feel different and unique, so visitors would feel like they were stepping into a whole new world as they moved from one part of the park to another. There was Main Street, U.S.A., inspired by the small American towns from the early 1900s; Adventureland, filled with jungle themes and exciting explorations; Fantasyland, where the stories and characters from Disney movies would come to life; Frontierland, with a Wild West theme; and Tomorrowland, a futuristic world that looked forward to what the future might hold.

Walt Disney faced many challenges along the way. Building Disneyland was incredibly expensive, and Walt had to get creative with funding. He even struck a deal with a television network, ABC, to create a TV show called *Disneyland*, which helped promote the park and also gave Walt the money he needed to keep building it. This show was very popular and introduced people across America to Disneyland even before it opened. Walt himself appeared on TV, explaining what each part of Disneyland would be like, and it got people excited to visit.

Through this show, people began to understand Walt's vision and to feel the magic he was creating.

Finally, after years of hard work, Disneyland was ready to open on July 17, 1955. Walt called it "Dedication Day," and it was one of the biggest events of the year. Thousands of people attended the opening, including celebrities, reporters, and regular families who were just as excited to see Disneyland for the first time. Walt Disney himself gave a speech, saying that Disneyland was meant to be a place "where age relives fond memories of the past and youth may savor the challenge and promise of the future." Disneyland was different from anything anyone had ever seen before. It wasn't just a park with rides; it was a place where people could feel like they were in a story, where characters came to life, and where every corner held a new adventure.

However, opening day wasn't as smooth as Walt had hoped. There were some unexpected challenges, like the fact that it was one of the hottest days of the summer. Some of the cement on the walkways was still drying, so ladies in high heels got stuck! Drinking fountains didn't work because of a plumbing problem, and there were so many people that the lines were much longer than planned. But despite these setbacks, people fell in love with Disneyland from the very start. They could see the magic that Walt had created, and many wanted to return as soon as they left.

Walt Disney continued to improve and expand Disneyland even after it opened. He was always coming up with new ideas and ways to make the park more exciting. He worked with his Imagineers to add new rides, new lands, and even more details to make the park feel real and enchanting. Walt's dream grew bigger each year, and he often walked through the park himself, talking to visitors and watching how they enjoyed each ride and attraction. He always wanted to make sure that Disneyland remained a place of happiness and wonder.

Today, Disneyland is still one of the most beloved places in the world. Millions of people visit from all over the globe to experience the magic that Walt dreamed of so long ago. Even though Walt Disney himself passed away in 1966, his dream continues. His ideas and passion live on in every ride, every parade, and every magical moment in the park. Disneyland has expanded with new lands and attractions, keeping Walt's original vision alive while adding new stories and characters from modern Disney films. But the heart of Disneyland—the magic, the sense of wonder, and the joy of being together with family—remains just as Walt Disney dreamed it would be. It's a place where imagination has no limits, where people of all ages can feel like kids again, and where every visit brings a new adventure.

Chapter 3: A Day in Disneyland; Where to Start

A day in Disneyland is like stepping into a dream where every corner of the park is filled with something amazing to see, do, or taste! Planning a day at Disneyland can make the experience even more magical, especially since there's so much to explore. First, start by arriving early to get the most out of your day. Gates open well before the rides, so you can soak up the atmosphere on Main Street, U.S.A., grab a tasty snack like a warm churro or Mickey-shaped pretzel, and start the day with excitement.

The best place to begin is Main Street, U.S.A., which looks like a charming town from a long time ago. This street is filled with cute shops, delicious bakeries, and friendly people. One of the first things you'll see when you walk in is the giant Mickey floral design, made out of beautiful flowers, which is perfect for a photo! If you have a map, take a moment to check out the layout of the park and decide which lands you want to visit first. Many people like to head straight to Sleeping Beauty Castle, the shining centerpiece of Disneyland, and it's a great spot to snap a picture to mark the start of your adventure. From there, you have a few exciting options: you could go to the left toward Adventureland and Frontierland, or to the right toward Tomorrowland, or walk straight into Fantasyland through the castle.

Adventureland is a thrilling place to start if you love exploring and discovering hidden treasures. It's filled with jungle vibes, and you can start your journey with the Jungle Cruise, a funny boat ride where a tour guide will make you laugh with jokes while you see "wild" animals (they're animatronic, but they look very real!). From there, you can head over to Indiana Jones Adventure, an exciting ride that makes you feel like you're racing through ancient temples alongside Indiana

Jones himself. It's a thrilling way to kick off the day, and it's perfect for adventurers!

If you're ready for some classic Disney fairytales, Fantasyland is where the magic of Disney movies comes to life. You'll find enchanting rides based on your favorite stories, like Peter Pan's Flight, where you soar over the city of London on a magical pirate ship! Don't miss Dumbo the Flying Elephant, a fun ride where you can control how high or low you fly in your very own Dumbo. Fantasyland also has the famous *It's a Small World*, where you take a boat ride through different scenes filled with singing dolls dressed in costumes from all over the world. The song will stick in your head all day, but it's a small price to pay for a delightful experience. There's also the Mad Tea Party, a classic spinning teacup ride that's tons of fun, especially if you don't mind a bit of a dizzy thrill. Fantasyland has plenty of attractions for everyone in the family, and it's a magical place to start your day if you're a fan of Disney characters and stories.

For those who love fast rides and futuristic themes, Tomorrowland is an exciting choice. You can race over to Space Mountain, a roller coaster in the dark that makes you feel like you're zooming through outer space. It's one of the most thrilling rides in the park and a favorite for anyone who loves a bit of adventure. Tomorrowland also has Buzz Lightyear Astro Blasters, a fun interactive ride where you can help Buzz save the galaxy by shooting targets as you ride along. Each person gets their own laser blaster, and you can compete with your friends or family to see who scores the highest! There's also Star Tours, a 3D adventure ride that takes you on a journey through the Star Wars universe, where you might meet characters like R2-D2 or fly past the Death Star. Tomorrowland feels like a glimpse into the future, and with all the amazing rides and high-tech attractions, it's a great place to start if you want some fast-paced fun.

Frontierland has a more rugged feel, like the Wild West. You can ride Big Thunder Mountain Railroad, which is like a runaway train zooming through caves and canyons. It's fast and bumpy, but it's loads of fun. There's also a large river where you can take a calm ride on the Mark Twain Riverboat, a beautiful steamboat that cruises along the Rivers of America. Frontierland is perfect for anyone who loves Western movies or dreams of being a cowboy or cowgirl. You might even catch a fun show with characters dressed up in cowboy hats and boots, adding to the old-timey feel of the land.

New Orleans Square is filled with the flavor and music of New Orleans, a city known for its jazz and charm. It's home to two of Disneyland's most popular attractions: the Haunted Mansion and Pirates of the Caribbean. The Haunted Mansion is a spooky (but not too scary!) ride through a haunted house filled with friendly ghosts. The ride has a mix of mystery and humor, with dancing ghosts, floating candles, and even a singing statue! Pirates of the Caribbean is a boat ride through scenes of pirate treasure, pirate battles, and a little pirate mischief. You'll see treasure chests, pirate skeletons, and maybe even Captain Jack Sparrow himself! New Orleans Square is also a fantastic place to try some delicious food like beignets (fried doughnuts covered in powdered sugar) or gumbo. It's a must-visit area if you're looking for a mix of adventure and a touch of spooky fun.

Critter Country is a cozy, woodsy area that's home to some lovable animal friends. One of the main attractions here is Splash Mountain, a thrilling log ride based on the tales of Br'er Rabbit, with a big splash at the end that might leave you a little wet! It's especially fun on a warm day, and if you're up for a bit of excitement, it's a ride you won't want to miss. You'll also find The Many Adventures of Winnie the Pooh, a gentle ride perfect for younger visitors, where you can join Pooh and his friends on a honey-filled adventure.

As the day goes on, make sure to take a break and grab some food. Disneyland has so many fun snacks, from giant turkey legs to corn dogs, churros, popcorn, and even Mickey-shaped ice cream bars. If you're hungry for a meal, there are places with everything from burgers and fries to more adventurous meals like gumbo or fried chicken. Each land has its own food spots, so you can enjoy something unique to each area of the park. You might even spot some characters while you're eating, like Mickey, Minnie, or Goofy, who are always happy to wave or pose for a picture.

In the afternoon, as the sun starts to set, you might want to find a good spot for the parade. Disneyland parades are amazing shows filled with colorful floats, music, and characters waving to the crowd. It's a chance to see all your favorite Disney characters up close as they dance and sing their way down Main Street. And when night falls, the magic isn't over yet. There's often a spectacular fireworks show over Sleeping Beauty Castle, lighting up the sky with beautiful colors, and it feels like the perfect end to a perfect day.

Disneyland has something for everyone, and the best way to enjoy your day is to go with the flow, be open to surprises, and follow the magic wherever it leads you. There are so many hidden details, friendly cast members (the people who work at Disneyland), and little moments of magic that pop up all day. You might find a character drawing pictures on the street with water, or a musician playing a lively tune. Every visit to Disneyland feels different because there's always something new to discover. So, start with the rides and lands you're most excited about, keep an eye out for shows and parades, and remember that the most magical days are often the ones that are filled with a little adventure and a lot of fun!

Chapter 4: Main Street's Hidden Surprises

Main Street, U.S.A., is the charming entrance to Disneyland, welcoming everyone into a magical world. At first glance, it looks like a quaint, old-fashioned street from the early 1900s, with brick buildings, colorful shops, and horse-drawn carriages. But there's more to Main Street than meets the eye! Walt Disney designed this street with hidden surprises and clever details that bring it to life and make it feel extra special. Main Street might seem simple, but if you pay close attention, you'll find lots of secrets that most people miss on their first visit.

One of the first surprises is the way Main Street itself is designed to feel welcoming and familiar. The buildings are constructed with a trick called "forced perspective." This means that the lower floors of each building are built larger than the upper floors, creating an illusion that the buildings are taller than they actually are. As you walk down the street, the buildings seem grand and impressive, but not so tall that they feel overwhelming. This clever trick makes you feel cozy and comfortable, like you're in a friendly, small town where everyone knows each other.

Keep an eye out for the windows on Main Street, too, because they are filled with little secrets. Many of the windows have names on them, and each one is a tribute to a person who helped create Disneyland or played a big role in the Disney company. These windows look like advertisements for different businesses, but each name represents someone who made Disneyland possible. For example, you might spot a window dedicated to Walt Disney's brother, Roy O. Disney, who helped Walt make his dream of Disneyland a reality by handling the finances. There's even a window for Walt Disney himself, showing his love for the park he created. These windows are like a hidden "Hall of Fame" for Disney legends, and each name has its own story.

Another wonderful hidden detail on Main Street is the smell. Disneyland uses a device called the "Smellitzer" to pump out delicious scents that make Main Street feel cozy and inviting. Near the bakery, you might smell fresh-baked cookies or warm cinnamon rolls, even if nothing is actually baking at the moment. This delightful smell draws people into the shops and makes the whole street feel like a place you want to explore. The Smellitzer changes scents depending on the season, so in the fall, you might catch the smell of pumpkin spice, and during the winter holidays, you might smell peppermint or gingerbread. This clever detail adds to the magical feeling of Main Street, making it feel like a real place where people live and work.

One of the most special hidden surprises is Walt Disney's personal touch on Main Street. In one of the windows above the fire station, you'll see a small lamp that's always lit. This lamp was a special tradition started by Walt Disney himself. Whenever Walt was at Disneyland, he would stay in a small apartment above the fire station, and he would leave the lamp on so people would know he was there. After he passed away, Disney decided to keep the lamp lit to honor his memory, as if to say Walt is always present in Disneyland, watching over the park he loved so much. For many Disney fans, this lamp is a touching reminder of Walt's legacy and his dream to create a place of joy for everyone.

As you walk down Main Street, listen closely, and you might hear some surprising sounds. Disney Imagineers, who design the parks, added hidden sounds to bring Main Street to life. For example, if you stand near the dentist's office, you might hear the sound of a patient groaning and the dentist working with his tools. Near a dance studio, you might hear the sound of tap dancing. Each sound is like a mini story, adding to the feeling that Main Street is a real, bustling town. These hidden sound effects are easy to miss, but once you notice them, they make the street feel even more alive and exciting.

Main Street also has hidden symbols, known as "Hidden Mickeys," throughout its design. Hidden Mickeys are small images of Mickey

Mouse's head that are carefully placed in different areas of the park for people to find. They're like a secret treasure hunt, and Main Street has quite a few if you know where to look! For example, you might find a Hidden Mickey in the ironwork on a balcony or in the decorations on a shop sign. These little Mickey shapes are scattered around the park and are a fun challenge for those who want to spot them all. Each Hidden Mickey is like a little reminder of Disney magic, hidden in plain sight for those who take the time to look.

If you peek into the shops along Main Street, you'll find even more surprises. Some shops have unique decorations that tell their own stories. The Emporium, one of the biggest stores on Main Street, has display windows that show scenes from classic Disney movies. These scenes change over time, so each visit might show something new. Some shops even have special displays related to Disneyland history, like old tickets or photos from Disneyland's opening day. And if you look closely in some windows, you might spot a small figure of a character waving at you or doing something funny, as if they're alive and part of the world of Main Street.

There's also a magic mailbox! At the Main Street Post Office, if you drop a postcard or letter in the mailbox, it will actually get sent. Imagine sending a postcard from Disneyland that arrives with a special Disneyland postmark. For many visitors, mailing a postcard from Disneyland is a fun way to share a bit of the magic with friends or family back home. And if you look at the address signs on Main Street buildings, you'll notice that some of them match important years in Disney history, like the year Walt was born or the year Disneyland opened.

Main Street doesn't have big rides like some of the other lands, but it does have the Main Street vehicles, which are special in their own way. You can ride on a horse-drawn streetcar, an old-fashioned fire engine, or a vintage double-decker bus. These vehicles add to the charm and feel of the street, and each one has its own style and details that make you feel like you've traveled back in time. The drivers of these vehicles often tell fun facts about Disneyland, so hopping on one of these rides is a great way to learn something new and experience Main Street from a different view.

At different times of day, you'll also find surprise performances on Main Street. The Dapper Dans, a barbershop quartet, often stroll down the street singing in perfect harmony. Their songs are cheerful, and they add to the lively atmosphere of Main Street. Sometimes, the Disneyland Band or other musical groups also perform, filling the street with music. And during special times of year, like Halloween or Christmas, Main Street is decorated with festive lights, banners, and decorations that add a whole new layer of magic.

Main Street is filled with so many hidden surprises that even people who have been to Disneyland many times discover new things every visit. It's not just a street you walk through to get to the rides; it's a world of its own, with layers of details, history, and little bits of magic tucked away for those who take the time to look. Every shop, window, and corner has a story, and these hidden surprises make Main Street feel like a place that's alive with memories and imagination.

Chapter 5: Adventure Awaits in Adventureland

Adventureland is one of the most thrilling and mysterious parts of Disneyland, designed to make you feel like you're journeying to exotic places filled with jungles, rivers, and hidden treasures. It's perfect for anyone with a spirit of adventure and curiosity! From the moment you step into Adventureland, you're surrounded by lush greenery, tall palm trees, and sounds of birds and jungle animals that make you feel like you're deep in a faraway land. Every detail is carefully planned to make this place feel like a real jungle, and even the air seems warmer and filled with the scent of tropical plants. Adventureland is like stepping into an adventure movie, and it's a land with some of the park's most unique and exciting attractions.

One of the first attractions you'll come across in Adventureland is the Jungle Cruise, a classic Disneyland ride that takes you on a hilarious boat trip through different "exotic" rivers from around the world. The Jungle Cruise is one of Disneyland's original rides and has been entertaining visitors since the park first opened in 1955. As you board the boat, a friendly guide or "skipper" will greet you and take you on a tour through rivers filled with animatronic animals, including elephants, crocodiles, lions, and gorillas. The skipper makes funny jokes and silly puns along the way, so you'll be laughing just as much as you're admiring the scenery. You'll see a "sleeping" tiger on the banks, a group of explorers climbing a pole to escape a rhino, and even a group of gorillas causing mischief with camping supplies. The Jungle Cruise is both funny and exciting, and the skippers' jokes are different every time, so you never know what to expect. Each skipper brings their own personality to the ride, so every trip feels a little different.

Another incredible attraction in Adventureland is the Indiana Jones Adventure, also known as *Indiana Jones and the Temple of the*

Forbidden Eye. This ride is like stepping into an Indiana Jones movie, filled with suspense, adventure, and a touch of danger. The story is that you're joining Indiana Jones on a journey to explore a mysterious temple. As you enter, the temple itself is dark and filled with strange carvings and ancient artifacts, which makes it feel like a real archaeological site. The line for this ride is part of the experience, as you walk through dark tunnels filled with booby traps and treasures. The atmosphere builds excitement and makes you feel like a true adventurer before you even get on the ride.

Once you board the special "jeep" vehicle, the adventure truly begins. The Indiana Jones Adventure is a high-speed ride that twists and turns as you encounter traps, giant snakes, lava pits, and even a huge boulder that seems to roll toward you just like in the Indiana Jones movies. Special effects make everything feel realistic, from the creepy crawlies on the walls to the flashes of light that reveal ancient carvings. This ride is intense and filled with surprises, and it's one of the most thrilling experiences in Disneyland. If you love adventure stories or Indiana Jones movies, this ride will be one of your favorites in Adventureland.

Adventureland isn't just about thrilling rides, though—it's also home to the Enchanted Tiki Room, a unique attraction that offers a completely different kind of experience. The Enchanted Tiki Room is a charming indoor show filled with singing animatronic birds, flowers, and tikis. When you enter, it feels like stepping into a tropical paradise, with decorations inspired by Polynesian culture. As the show begins, the lights dim, and the room comes alive with music. Birds with colorful feathers start singing and telling jokes, and even the carved wooden tikis join in! This show is a favorite for all ages because it's relaxing, funny, and has catchy tunes that are hard to forget. One of the most famous songs from the Tiki Room is "The Tiki, Tiki, Tiki Room," and it's so lively that many people leave singing it as they walk out. The

Tiki Room is a great place to rest and enjoy some air conditioning, while still feeling the spirit of Adventureland.

Right outside the Tiki Room, you'll find one of Disneyland's most famous snacks: Dole Whip! Dole Whip is a creamy, pineapple-flavored soft serve that's cool and refreshing, especially on a hot day. You can get it plain or as a float with pineapple juice. It's one of the most popular treats in Adventureland, and many visitors say no trip to Disneyland is complete without enjoying a Dole Whip. This little spot near the Tiki Room often has a line because people love Dole Whip so much, but it's worth the wait. Eating a Dole Whip while relaxing under the tropical trees around the Tiki Room just adds to the magic of Adventureland.

Adventureland also has some unique shops that are filled with treasures from around the world. One of the most interesting shops is called the Adventureland Bazaar. It's decorated with artifacts and items that look like they came from a distant jungle or ancient temple. Here, you can find everything from safari hats and tiki mugs to unique souvenirs like carved animals or tropical-themed clothing. It feels like a small, hidden market you'd find in the middle of a jungle expedition. Even if you're not buying anything, it's fun to wander around and check out all the different items. The shop is filled with details that make it feel like part of an adventure, and sometimes you might even find a cast member telling stories or showing cool items from the "jungle" nearby.

If you're looking to relax or need a place to sit down and plan your next adventure, Adventureland has a little spot called Tropical Hideaway. It's a cozy outdoor area where you can grab a snack, sit by the water, and watch the Jungle Cruise boats float by. This area is decorated with tropical plants, colorful lanterns, and little details that make it feel like an explorer's camp. You can also try new treats here, like bao buns and other tasty bites inspired by flavors from around the world. The Tropical Hideaway is a great place to recharge, soak up the jungle atmosphere, and maybe even catch a glimpse of Rosita, a friendly animatronic cockatoo who loves to chat with visitors and make jokes.

Adventureland comes alive with little surprises and hidden details if you take the time to explore. The whole area feels like a journey through different parts of the world, filled with mysteries waiting to be uncovered. You might notice carvings or statues that look like they came from ancient civilizations, or hear drums and exotic music playing in the background. Even the trash cans are decorated with adventure-themed designs! Every corner of Adventureland is thoughtfully designed to make you feel like an explorer, and sometimes cast members will even get into character, acting as if they're guides on a real expedition.

In Adventureland, you'll also come across hidden symbols called "Hidden Mickeys," which are little images of Mickey Mouse's head hidden in the decorations. These are part of a secret "treasure hunt" all over Disneyland, and Adventureland has a few if you look carefully. You might spot a Hidden Mickey in the carvings on a wall, in the stones near the Jungle Cruise, or even in the pattern on a tiki decoration. Finding these Hidden Mickeys adds to the sense of exploration, as you uncover small Disney surprises hidden within the adventure.

At night, Adventureland becomes even more mysterious and magical. The lights are dimmed, and the area glows with warm, flickering torches and lanterns. Shadows make the jungle plants and statues look even more mysterious, and the sounds of the jungle feel deeper and more enchanting. The nighttime atmosphere in Adventureland makes it feel like a whole new adventure, perfect for those who want to experience the thrill of exploring the unknown. Walking through Adventureland at night is like stepping into a storybook filled with mystery, where anything could happen.

Adventureland is more than just a place for rides—it's a whole world of exploration, fun, and discovery. Every time you visit, there's something new to notice, whether it's a small detail on a statue, a new joke from the Jungle Cruise skipper, or an unusual souvenir in the

Bazaar. Adventureland lets you live out your own adventure, complete with thrilling rides, friendly characters, hidden treasures, and delicious treats. It's a place where imagination runs wild, and every step brings a new surprise. For those who love stories of exploration and excitement, Adventureland is the ultimate destination in Disneyland, where adventure truly awaits around every corner.

Chapter 6: Exploring Fantasyland's Fairy Tales

Fantasyland is one of the most enchanting places in Disneyland, filled with the magic and wonder of classic fairy tales. When you step into Fantasyland, it's like walking right into the pages of a storybook. Colorful castles, charming cottages, and cobblestone paths make it feel like a fantasy world where anything is possible. Fantasyland is home to some of the most beloved characters and stories, and everywhere you look, there's something to remind you of the magical tales you've read or watched in movies. From princes and princesses to mystical creatures and magical lands, Fantasyland brings these stories to life with amazing detail, and it feels like every corner has a new story waiting to be discovered.

The heart of Fantasyland is Sleeping Beauty Castle, which stands tall and elegant, decorated with pink and blue spires that sparkle in the sun. The castle is based on the one from *Sleeping Beauty*, and it's the centerpiece of the whole park. You can walk right through the castle's arched entrance and even explore some of the rooms inside. There's a small, hidden attraction called the Sleeping Beauty Castle Walkthrough, where you can see scenes from the *Sleeping Beauty* story brought to life with beautiful displays and lights. It's like getting a peek into Aurora's story, and if you listen closely, you might hear music from the movie or even a hint of Maleficent's laugh echoing through the halls. For many people, visiting the castle is one of the highlights of Fantasyland, as it truly feels like stepping into a fairy tale.

Fantasyland is filled with classic rides based on beloved Disney movies, and each ride takes you right into the heart of the story. One of the most popular rides is *Peter Pan's Flight*, where you can board a pirate ship and "fly" over London and Neverland. The ride begins with Tinker Bell sprinkling pixie dust on your ship, and then you soar into the night sky, looking down on tiny models of London's Big Ben and the glittering Thames River. Soon, you're flying over Neverland, where you'll see Captain Hook, the Lost Boys, and even a giant crocodile snapping his jaws. The ride is short but incredibly magical, making you feel like you're really flying alongside Peter Pan and Wendy. Because of its popularity, *Peter Pan's Flight* often has a long line, but many fans say the wait is worth it to experience the magic of flying.

Another enchanting ride is *Snow White's Enchanted Wish*, which tells the story of *Snow White and the Seven Dwarfs*. You board a small mine cart and travel through scenes from the classic movie. From the start, you can feel the warmth of Snow White's character as she dances and sings with her animal friends. As the ride goes on, you encounter the Evil Queen and her magic mirror, making the atmosphere a bit darker and more mysterious. There's even a spooky moment where you pass by the Queen's laboratory, where she's brewing her potion to transform into the old hag. But the story ends on a happy note, with Snow White finding true love and being reunited with her prince. The ride captures the ups and downs of Snow White's story, mixing moments of danger with the warmth and joy of true love.

One of the most cheerful rides in Fantasyland is *It's a Small World*, a gentle boat ride that takes you through scenes from all around the world. The attraction is filled with dolls dressed in traditional costumes from different countries, and they all sing the famous "It's a Small World" song. Each scene is brightly colored and filled with details that show the unique cultures and landscapes of different places. You'll see everything from Paris's Eiffel Tower to Mount Fuji in Japan, and even tropical islands and desert scenes. The dolls are designed with happy faces, and the song they sing is all about friendship and unity, making the ride feel like a celebration of peace and togetherness. The ride's colorful artwork and joyful message make it a favorite for kids and families, and it's especially magical during the holidays when it's decorated with lights and Christmas music.

Fantasyland is also home to *Mr. Toad's Wild Ride*, a fast-paced, whimsical journey based on *The Wind in the Willows*. This ride is unlike any other in Disneyland because it takes you on a "wild ride" through Mr. Toad's life, with sharp turns and silly surprises around every corner. You hop into a small motorcar and zoom through scenes of Toad Hall, the countryside, and even a run-in with the police! The ride's design is full of humor and unexpected moments, and it's a favorite for those who enjoy a little bit of chaos and fun. *Mr. Toad's Wild Ride* is one of the original Disneyland attractions, and it's beloved for its unique story and playful energy.

Another classic is *Alice in Wonderland*, which brings Lewis Carroll's famous story to life. You ride in a caterpillar-shaped car and journey through Wonderland, meeting characters like the White Rabbit, Cheshire Cat, and the Queen of Hearts. The ride is filled with bright colors, strange shapes, and whimsical scenes that capture the imagination. From the Mad Hatter's tea party to the Queen's giant roses, each scene is packed with quirky details that make Wonderland feel wonderfully bizarre. The ride feels like stepping into a dream where anything can happen, just like in the story of *Alice in Wonderland*.

Fantasyland also has a beautiful carousel called *King Arthur Carrousel*, which has horses carved in intricate detail and decorated in rich colors. This carousel is inspired by the stories of King Arthur, and each horse has its own personality and design. As you ride, you'll hear cheerful music that makes the carousel feel like a timeless fairy-tale moment. Kids love picking their favorite horse to ride, and some visitors even say that one of the horses, called "Jingles," is enchanted! Jingles has golden bells and special decorations that make it stand out, and it's said to be dedicated to Walt Disney's wife, Lillian. Riding the carousel is a simple joy, but it adds to the magic of Fantasyland.

Fantasyland is full of delightful little details that make the whole land feel alive. The shops and restaurants look like they belong in a fairy-tale village, with thatched roofs, stained glass windows, and colorful flags. One popular spot to visit is the *Mad Hatter*, a hat shop filled with playful hats inspired by Disney characters, including the famous Mickey Mouse ears. Another fun shop is *Castle Holiday Shoppe*, which is filled with Christmas ornaments and decorations all year long, making it feel like a little piece of holiday magic right in the middle of Fantasyland. For those who love sweets, *Maurice's Treats* offers tasty snacks like twisted churros and refreshing drinks that add to the joyful atmosphere.

Characters are a big part of Fantasyland's magic, too. You might see Peter Pan dashing around, looking for his shadow, or Snow White chatting with her animal friends. Cinderella, Ariel, and other princesses often make appearances, greeting fans and taking photos. Meeting these characters in Fantasyland is like seeing them in their own story worlds, and it's a chance to talk to your favorite Disney characters face-to-face. For many kids, this is one of the most exciting parts of Fantasyland because it feels like the characters have stepped right out of the movies to share a special moment with you.

At night, Fantasyland transforms into an even more magical place. The lights on Sleeping Beauty Castle twinkle, and the whole area glows with warm, inviting colors. Sometimes there are fireworks above the castle, making it look like a scene from a fairy tale. The reflections of the lights on the water near *It's a Small World* create a dreamy atmosphere, and the rides feel even more enchanting. Fantasyland at night is quieter and feels like a place of pure magic, as if the stories are all coming to life under the starlit sky. Many visitors say that riding *Peter Pan's Flight* or strolling through Fantasyland at night is an unforgettable experience.

Fantasyland isn't just a place with rides; it's a celebration of the stories and characters that Disney fans have loved for generations. Every detail, from the architecture to the music, is designed to make you feel like you've stepped into a magical world where dreams really do come true. Whether it's flying over Neverland, exploring a spooky forest, or simply walking through the peaceful village square,

Fantasyland is a place where fairy tales come alive in the most enchanting way possible. For anyone who believes in the magic of stories, Fantasyland is a world of endless wonder, waiting to be explored again and again.

Chapter 7: Thrills in Tomorrowland's Future World

Tomorrowland is a part of Disneyland where you get to experience the wonders of the future and dive into the excitement of space travel, futuristic cities, and advanced technology. Stepping into Tomorrowland feels like entering a different world where science fiction meets reality, and every corner is filled with exciting things to discover. With sleek metal buildings, flashing lights, and futuristic sounds, the atmosphere in Tomorrowland makes you feel like you're on a space station or part of a high-tech city from the future. It's the perfect spot for anyone who loves fast-paced thrills, robots, and the mysteries of outer space. Tomorrowland is also one of the most action-packed areas of Disneyland, with thrilling rides and attractions that let you explore space, race through time, and even team up with superheroes to save the world.

One of the most thrilling rides in Tomorrowland is *Space Mountain*, a roller coaster that takes you on a high-speed journey through outer space. As you wait in line, you'll see displays about stars, planets, and galaxies, setting the stage for your space mission. Once you board the sleek spaceship, you're blasted off into a dark tunnel filled with flashing lights and sounds of engines powering up. Suddenly, you're racing through the dark void of space, dodging asteroids and flying past stars at lightning speed. The ride is completely indoors and almost entirely in the dark, so it feels like you're truly out in space, zooming through the universe. With twists, turns, and sudden drops, *Space Mountain* is both thrilling and slightly mysterious, making it a favorite for adventure-seekers who want to experience the excitement of space travel without ever leaving Earth. The feeling of weightlessness combined with the intense speed creates an experience like no other, and every time you ride it, you'll feel like a true space explorer.

Another must-see attraction in Tomorrowland is *Star Tours: The Adventures Continue*, a 3D motion-simulator ride that's all about the galaxy far, far away from the *Star Wars* movies. When you enter *Star Tours*, you're treated like a traveler about to board a spaceship to visit different planets in the *Star Wars* universe. The waiting area is designed to look like a futuristic spaceport, complete with droids and alien creatures bustling about. When it's your turn, you'll board a transport ship and wear special 3D glasses for an immersive experience. Suddenly, you're on an adventure with characters like C-3PO, R2-D2, and other heroes from the *Star Wars* saga. The ride is unpredictable, with different destinations and scenes each time, so you might find yourself dodging Imperial forces, racing across icy planets, or facing off against the Dark Side. The realistic visuals, combined with the movement of the simulator, make you feel like you're truly in the middle of a *Star Wars* battle. This ride is thrilling and perfect for fans of the *Star Wars* universe or anyone who wants to explore otherworldly destinations in the galaxy.

Tomorrowland is also home to *Buzz Lightyear Astro Blasters*, a ride where you get to be a part of Buzz Lightyear's Star Command team from *Toy Story*. In this interactive ride, you help Buzz defeat the evil Emperor Zurg by aiming and shooting at targets with a laser gun. Each time you hit a target, you earn points, and the more points you score, the closer you get to being a "Galactic Hero." As you move through the ride, you'll encounter aliens, robots, and spaceships that are all part of Zurg's plan to take over the universe. *Buzz Lightyear Astro Blasters* is a lot of fun because it combines the excitement of a game with the thrill of a ride, and you can compete with your friends and family to see who can get the highest score. The colorful lights, cheerful music, and playful animations make it a perfect adventure for all ages, and it's especially fun for those who love interactive games.

One of Tomorrowland's coolest attractions is *Autopia*, where you can actually drive a car along a winding track that feels like a futuristic highway. *Autopia* has been a part of Disneyland since it opened in 1955, but it's been updated to feel more futuristic with eco-friendly themes and a sleek, modern look. Each car is designed to look like a futuristic vehicle, and though they're on tracks to keep you from going too far off course, you get to steer and control the speed of your car. Driving along the track, you'll see futuristic signs, robot-themed billboards, and even a little roadside scenery that makes it feel like a mini-road trip. It's a great ride for kids who want to feel like they're driving a real car and offers a unique experience since you're in control. Autopia also has a special smell – a mix of gasoline and rubber tires that adds to the feeling of being on a real highway. Although it's not as fast-paced as some of the other rides in Tomorrowland, Autopia is a classic experience that gives you a taste of driving in a world of tomorrow.

Finding Nemo Submarine Voyage is another unique adventure in Tomorrowland that takes you underwater. This ride uses real submarines that submerge underwater, making you feel like an explorer on a sea voyage. As you look out the submarine's windows, you'll see beautiful underwater scenes filled with coral reefs, sea plants, and schools of fish, all brought to life with special lighting and sound effects. Suddenly, you'll spot characters from *Finding Nemo*, like Nemo, Dory, and Marlin, who are on their own adventure right alongside you. This ride blends real scenery with animated projections, creating a magical underwater world that feels alive with sea creatures and mysterious caves. The gentle motion of the submarine, combined with the colorful and detailed scenery, makes this ride feel like an underwater safari, and it's perfect for anyone who loves ocean adventures and Pixar's *Finding Nemo*.

For those interested in cutting-edge technology and science, *Star Wars: Launch Bay* offers a space filled with cool exhibits, models, and artifacts from the *Star Wars* galaxy. Here, you can check out costumes and props from the movies, and you might even meet characters like

Chewbacca, Darth Vader, or Boba Fett. The Launch Bay has displays that explain the technology and vehicles from *Star Wars*, so it's both entertaining and educational for fans who want to learn more about the galaxy's ships and gear. It's also a great place to take photos with your favorite characters or pose next to a life-sized X-wing fighter or speeder bike.

If you're looking for a thrill that combines speed, energy, and stunning visuals, *Hyperspace Mountain* is a special version of *Space Mountain* that's themed around *Star Wars*. In this version, you blast off into a space battle between the Rebels and the Empire, with X-wings and TIE fighters flying all around you. With intense music and flashing laser blasts, the ride feels even more like a high-speed escape through the galaxy. You'll hear commands from the Rebel Alliance as they guide you through the battle, and you might even come face-to-face with a Star Destroyer! This special version of *Space Mountain* only comes around sometimes, so it's a must-try for *Star Wars* fans when it's available.

Tomorrowland also has futuristic food spots that make you feel like you're dining in the future. At the *Galactic Grill*, you can find burgers, sandwiches, and treats that are given names inspired by space adventures. The decorations and seating areas make it feel like a cafeteria on a space station, with views of the Tomorrowland rides in the background. The *Alien Pizza Planet*, themed around the aliens from *Toy Story*, serves pizza and pasta in a colorful, space-themed environment. The seating area looks like a sci-fi cafeteria with rockets and alien decorations, and the food names add a playful touch to your meal. Dining in Tomorrowland is a part of the experience, as it feels like every food option is designed to match the futuristic theme of the land.

Another unique spot in Tomorrowland is *Tomorrowland Terrace*, which is a stage where you can watch live music performances. Sometimes, the stage even hosts *Jedi Training: Trials of the Temple*, a show where kids can learn how to wield a lightsaber and face off against

Darth Vader or the Inquisitor. Watching young Jedi trainees learn the ways of the Force is fun for everyone, and for kids who participate, it's an unforgettable experience to be trained by a Jedi and battle the Dark Side in front of a cheering crowd. It adds an interactive element to Tomorrowland, where kids can truly feel like heroes in their own *Star Wars* story.

As the sun sets, Tomorrowland takes on a different vibe, with lights glowing in blues, purples, and whites, making the futuristic architecture stand out even more. At night, the whole area feels like a real spaceport, and the lights on *Space Mountain* and *Star Tours* make them seem even more thrilling. The reflections of lights on the metallic surfaces of Tomorrowland create a high-tech, dreamy atmosphere that's perfect for exploring. Rides like *Buzz Lightyear Astro Blasters* feel even more exciting under the stars, and the soft glow of *Finding Nemo Submarine Voyage* adds to the magic.

Tomorrowland is a land that encourages curiosity, excitement, and dreams of the future. From exploring space to fighting alongside heroes, it's a place where imagination and technology come together to create unforgettable adventures. Whether you're battling for the galaxy, driving futuristic cars, or meeting droids, Tomorrowland offers something exciting for everyone. It's not just a glimpse into what the future might look like, but a place where everyone can experience the thrills of a world where technology and adventure come to life. For those who dream of exploring space, traveling at light speed, or just experiencing the wonders of what's yet to come, Tomorrowland is a destination that makes the future feel as thrilling as any adventure.

Chapter 8: Secrets of Frontierland's Wild West

Frontierland is Disneyland's very own slice of the Wild West, where visitors step into a world inspired by pioneers, cowboys, gold miners, and riverboats. When you enter Frontierland, you're transported to a time when the western frontier was still untamed and full of adventure. It's designed to feel like a small, bustling town on the edge of the wilderness, with wooden buildings, wagon wheels, and cacti all around. This land has exciting rides, hidden treasures, and loads of western charm that make you feel like a real explorer or cowboy discovering a new land. With thrilling attractions, rustic landscapes, and historical touches, Frontierland offers plenty of secrets to uncover, showing visitors a fascinating look at the adventures and challenges of the American frontier.

One of the most popular attractions in Frontierland is *Big Thunder Mountain Railroad*, often called the "wildest ride in the wilderness." This roller coaster is set in a spooky, abandoned mining town called Rainbow Ridge, where miners once struck gold. The story goes that the mountain is "cursed," and strange things started happening when miners tried to dig for too much gold too quickly. When you board the mine train, you're in for a thrilling journey through the mountain, passing by caves, waterfalls, and geysers. The ride is fast and filled with sudden turns and drops, making it feel like the runaway mine train is out of control. As you speed through the rocky terrain, you'll see animatronic animals like mountain goats and possums, as well as signs of the old mining operations, like wooden scaffolds and dynamite crates. In one part of the ride, you pass through a dark cavern filled with glittering crystals, and in another, you'll zoom past a field of erupting geysers. These little details create a sense of mystery around the old mining town, adding to the thrill of the ride. The mountain itself was designed to look like the famous red rock formations of Monument Valley, giving it a true Wild West feel.

Frontierland is also home to *The Mark Twain Riverboat*, a large, paddle-wheel riverboat that takes guests on a peaceful journey along the Rivers of America. The riverboat is a replica of the steamboats that used to travel up and down the Mississippi River, and it's named after Mark Twain, the famous American author who wrote about life on the river. As you ride, you can imagine what it might have been like to be a pioneer or an explorer heading into unknown territory. The riverboat takes you around Tom Sawyer Island and offers beautiful views of the wilderness areas around Frontierland. Along the riverbanks, you'll see animatronic animals like deer, moose, and Native American camps that add to the atmosphere. It's a calm and scenic ride, perfect for taking a break from the hustle and bustle of the park while enjoying the sights and sounds of the frontier.

Frontierland has its own hidden island, *Tom Sawyer Island*, named after the famous character from Mark Twain's book *The Adventures of Tom Sawyer*. To get to the island, you'll need to take a raft across the river, which is an adventure in itself! Once you're there, you can explore a network of caves, bridges, and secret trails that Tom and his friends might have explored. The island has plenty of fun, interactive spots, like Fort Wilderness, where you can pretend to be a soldier guarding the frontier, and Injun Joe's Cave, a mysterious cave that feels dark and a bit spooky. Kids love running around the island, discovering hidden treasures and acting out their own Wild West adventures. Tom Sawyer Island feels like a secret hideaway in the middle of Disneyland, where you can climb, explore, and play in a setting that feels straight out of a frontier story.

Frontierland has a lot of smaller details that make it feel like a real town from the Old West. For example, if you look closely at the Golden Horseshoe Saloon, you'll notice old-fashioned posters advertising live shows, just like in an old Western town. The Golden Horseshoe is a real saloon-style theater where you can watch musical performances and comedy shows while enjoying treats like ice cream and churros. It's designed with wooden balconies, red curtains, and paintings of cowboys, making you feel like you've stepped into a scene from an old Western movie. This saloon has a rich history in Disneyland, as it's one of the original attractions from when the park first opened in 1955. In the early days, Walt Disney himself used to host special performances here, making it a place full of Disneyland history.

In Frontierland, you'll also find the *Shooting Exposition*, a shooting gallery where you can try your hand at shooting targets, just like a real cowboy or frontiersman. The targets are designed to look like cans, bottles, and critters that you might find in the Wild West, and each time you hit one, it moves or makes a sound. This attraction has a lot of hidden details, like the sound effects that make you feel like you're in an old Western town. It's a fun, interactive experience that lets you feel like a sharpshooter from the frontier, and it's a great way to test your aim.

Frontierland is filled with historic touches that pay tribute to the American West. For example, many of the wooden buildings in Frontierland are designed to look like they're from the 1800s, with signs and decorations that make them look worn and weathered by the desert sun. Some of the signs have funny messages, like "Doc Wassell's Elixir of Life," hinting at the quirky medicine men who used to sell "miracle cures" in the Old West. If you look closely at the details on the buildings and shops, you'll see little clues about what life might have been like in a frontier town. For example, there's a blacksmith's shop with tools and horseshoes, and a trading post where you can imagine people would have bought supplies for their journeys across the frontier.

Another attraction that fits the Wild West theme is the *Sailing Ship Columbia*, a full-sized replica of the first American ship to sail around the world. This ship is docked near the riverboat and takes guests on a journey along the Rivers of America, where you can imagine what life was like for sailors and explorers in the 18th century. The ship is complete with sails, cannons, and a crew's quarters that you can explore. Sailing on the Columbia feels like going on an old-fashioned adventure, and the ship even fires its cannons during the trip, adding to the excitement. This attraction is great for learning a bit about history while enjoying the scenic views of Frontierland and beyond.

At night, Frontierland takes on a whole new look with the sounds of crickets and the sight of twinkling lanterns and campfires. If you visit during certain times of the year, you might catch the *Fantasmic!* show, an incredible nighttime performance on the Rivers of America. During this show, Mickey Mouse faces off against villains from Disney movies, and there are amazing water effects, fireworks, and even a giant fire-breathing dragon. The show takes place on the water near Frontierland and uses Tom Sawyer Island as a stage, creating a unique blend of storytelling and adventure. Fantasmic! is a fantastic way to end a day in Frontierland, as it combines the thrill of Disney magic with the natural beauty of the river.

Even the food in Frontierland is inspired by the flavors of the Wild West. At *Rancho del Zocalo*, a Mexican-style restaurant, you can find dishes like tacos, burritos, and churros, giving you a taste of the flavors that would have been enjoyed by settlers and explorers in the West. The restaurant has a cozy, adobe-style look, with colorful tiles, arches, and shaded outdoor seating that makes it feel like an authentic spot along the frontier. Another popular place to eat is the *River Belle Terrace*, where you can enjoy a view of the Rivers of America while feasting on BBQ dishes and Southern-inspired sides like cornbread and baked beans. These spots make Frontierland feel like a place where you can take a break from your adventures to enjoy a hearty meal, just like the pioneers might have done.

Throughout Frontierland, you'll also see cast members dressed in cowboy hats, bandanas, and boots, adding to the feeling of being in a real frontier town. These cast members sometimes act like characters from the Old West, sharing stories or acting like sheriffs or gold miners, which makes the experience even more immersive. They might greet you with a friendly "Howdy!" or tell you about the "gold rush" that hit the area, making it feel like the history of the frontier is alive all around you.

Frontierland is more than just rides and shows; it's an immersive world filled with history, mystery, and adventure. From the runaway trains of Big Thunder Mountain to the quiet wilderness of Tom Sawyer Island, there's always something new to discover in this land of the Old West. It's a place where kids and adults alike can imagine life as a pioneer or cowboy, and every visit brings the chance to uncover more secrets and hidden gems. Whether you're seeking thrills, exploring the wilderness, or enjoying a taste of frontier life, Frontierland is full of surprises that make it feel like you've truly traveled back to a time when the West was still wild.

Chapter 9: The Pirates of New Orleans Square

New Orleans Square in Disneyland is a magical place that feels like a step back in time to the lively streets of old New Orleans, where jazz music fills the air, gas lamps glow along cobblestone streets, and mysterious alleyways hint at hidden secrets. This area has an exciting blend of mystery, adventure, and history that makes it feel like an entirely different world within Disneyland. But one of the biggest draws to New Orleans Square is its connection to pirates and tales of buried treasure. Pirates have a huge presence here, and the legendary *Pirates of the Caribbean* ride is one of the most beloved attractions in Disneyland. Visitors are transported on a journey through spooky caves, pirate-infested waters, and ports under siege, making it feel like they're a part of an action-packed adventure in the Golden Age of Piracy.

When you approach *Pirates of the Caribbean*, you'll notice the dark and mysterious feel of the entrance, which looks like a dock leading into a hidden, haunted bay. The ride's building is designed to look like a grand yet slightly eerie mansion from the 1700s, complete with balconies and ironwork, making you feel like you're about to enter the lair of pirates. As you get closer, you might hear the faint sounds of splashing water, distant cannon fire, and the haunting tune of "Yo Ho (A Pirate's Life for Me)" coming from inside, setting the stage for an epic journey. The adventure begins the moment you board your boat, which glides away from the dock and into the dark, mysterious depths of the pirate-infested Caribbean.

The first part of the ride is eerily quiet, taking you through dark caves where ancient pirate treasures lie hidden among skulls, swords, and decaying wooden chests overflowing with gold coins and jewels. There's a ghostly feeling in the air as you pass by skeletons of pirates who, it seems, didn't survive the search for treasure. In one iconic scene, a skeleton pirate sits at the helm of a shipwreck, gripping the wheel with his bony hands as he stares out at the dark sea—a spooky reminder of the dangers of a pirate's life. This section of the ride gives you a glimpse into the greed and mystery of pirate legends, where those who chase riches sometimes meet a dangerous fate.

Soon, your boat glides down a waterfall, dropping into the heart of the pirate world. This plunge adds a burst of excitement and brings you directly into the middle of a thrilling pirate battle scene. Cannons fire back and forth between a pirate ship and a fortress, and you can hear the captain shouting orders to his crew. The smell of gunpowder fills the air as cannonballs splash into the water around you, making it feel like you're caught in the crossfire. This immersive scene captures the chaos and excitement of pirate life, showing just how daring and dangerous these outlaws of the sea could be. The pirate ship is enormous, with a fearsome black flag waving from the top, and animatronic pirates scramble around the deck, ready for action.

As the journey continues, your boat drifts into a town that has been captured by pirates, and it's here that you see the playful, mischievous side of these swashbuckling characters. The streets are lined with colorful buildings, and you'll spot pirates drinking, singing, and causing mayhem as they celebrate their victory. In one scene, pirates chase townspeople in circles around buildings, while in another, a group of pirates are gathered around a map, arguing over who gets which share of the treasure. The details here are incredible—there are barrels spilling out rum, lanterns flickering in the windows, and small animals like pigs and chickens wandering around the scene, all adding to the atmosphere of a lively pirate town. The characters are all animatronics, but their movements and expressions are so lifelike that it feels like you're witnessing a real pirate takeover.

One of the most memorable scenes in *Pirates of the Caribbean* features a group of pirates locked up in jail, trying to bribe a dog holding the key in his mouth. They reach through the bars, offering him bones and calling to him, hoping he'll come close enough to grab the key. This scene has become iconic and is a favorite among guests, capturing both the humor and desperation of pirate life. The dog, completely unaware of his importance, just looks at them with a stubborn expression, and the scene never fails to make people laugh. This mix of humor and adventure is one of the things that makes *Pirates of the Caribbean* so unique; it's not just about action and danger, but also about the silly, unpredictable world of pirates.

One interesting fact about the *Pirates of the Caribbean* ride is that it was one of the last attractions that Walt Disney personally worked on before he passed away. He wanted it to be something truly special, an attraction that would stand out for its attention to detail, storytelling, and immersive experience. Originally, the ride was supposed to be a walk-through wax museum, but as technology improved, Disney decided to make it a boat ride filled with animatronic characters. This decision changed the entire experience and allowed for a much more thrilling adventure. The ride became an instant classic when it opened in 1967, and it's been beloved by Disneyland visitors ever since. Over the years, some new elements have been added, including characters like Captain Jack Sparrow from the *Pirates of the Caribbean* movies, which brought a fresh twist to the story without changing its classic charm.

New Orleans Square itself is full of pirate-themed details that add to the feeling that you're in a world of hidden treasures and secret adventures. As you walk through the area, keep an eye out for hints that pirates may have passed through, like treasure maps hidden in shop windows or symbols of skulls and crossbones carved into the architecture. In one of the stores, *Pieces of Eight*, you'll find all kinds of pirate-themed souvenirs, from hats and swords to treasure chests and coins. It feels like a store where real pirates might have bought supplies before setting out on their next voyage. The atmosphere of

New Orleans Square, with its narrow alleyways and mysterious nooks, adds to the feeling that there are secrets hidden everywhere, just waiting to be discovered by curious explorers.

There's even a restaurant in New Orleans Square called *Blue Bayou*, where you can dine on delicious Creole-inspired dishes right beside the waters of *Pirates of the Caribbean*. Inside the Blue Bayou, the lights are dimmed to create the feeling of an evening under a starry sky, with lanterns hanging from trees and the quiet sound of crickets in the air. As you eat, you can watch boats from the ride float by, with guests just beginning their pirate adventure. Dining here makes you feel like you're part of the ride itself, as if you're in a cozy little town along the bay, enjoying a meal while pirates scheme nearby. This unique setting makes the Blue Bayou one of the most popular and memorable dining spots in Disneyland, offering a perfect blend of food and atmosphere.

In New Orleans Square, you might also stumble upon pirates wandering the streets or telling tales of their latest adventures. Sometimes, you'll see Jack Sparrow himself, sneaking around the area and stopping to chat with guests, sharing tips on how to be a pirate. He might even show you a few tricks or teach you how to say a proper pirate "Arrr!" Jack Sparrow's playful antics and sense of humor make him a fan-favorite, and it's always a thrill to spot him in New Orleans Square.

The pirate magic in New Orleans Square doesn't end with the rides and characters, though. The land is filled with small details that bring the pirate legend to life. There's a small, unmarked alley known as Royal Street, where you can find secret doors and balconies that hint at a hidden world of mystery. Some say there are clues in New Orleans Square that lead to hidden treasure, and if you're lucky, you might spot symbols or markings that look like they could be part of an old pirate map. Even the music you hear in New Orleans Square—gentle jazz tunes mixed with the occasional pirate chant—adds to the feeling that this place is full of secrets, waiting to be uncovered by those brave enough to search for them.

For fans of Disney's *Pirates of the Caribbean* movies, New Orleans Square is the perfect place to relive the excitement of the films. The ride inspired the movies, and then the movies inspired updates to the ride, creating a fun cycle of storytelling that brings both to life. The addition of characters like Jack Sparrow and Captain Barbossa to the ride means that fans can actually come face-to-face with their favorite pirate characters, making the experience even more magical.

New Orleans Square, with its blend of mystery, adventure, and historic charm, is one of Disneyland's most unique areas. From the haunting caves filled with pirate skeletons to the lively pirate towns, every corner of *Pirates of the Caribbean* tells a story, and each visit offers something new to discover. It's a place where the thrill of adventure and the mystery of hidden treasures come to life, inviting everyone to step into a world where pirates ruled the seas and treasure was only a daring journey away.

Chapter 10: Ride Guide; The Must-Do Attractions

A trip to Disneyland isn't complete without experiencing some of its most iconic attractions—the must-do rides that bring the magic of the park to life and create memories you'll never forget. With so many incredible options, it can be tricky to know where to start, but there are a few attractions that stand out as absolute essentials. From thrilling coasters and immersive adventures to enchanting boat rides and high-tech journeys, Disneyland has something for everyone, and each ride brings a different kind of wonder and excitement. Whether you're visiting for the first time or you're a Disneyland pro, this guide will give you an idea of the rides you simply can't miss.

One of the first stops on any must-do list is *Pirates of the Caribbean*. This classic water ride takes you on a journey through the world of pirates, complete with treasure-filled caves, eerie skeletons, and bustling pirate towns. As your boat glides through different scenes, you'll see pirates singing, dancing, and causing mischief, making it feel like you're in the middle of a real pirate adventure. The ride has been thrilling visitors for decades and is filled with so much detail that every trip offers something new to discover. From the iconic "Yo Ho (A Pirate's Life for Me)" song to the mysterious caves and battles, this attraction sets the mood for an unforgettable Disneyland experience.

Just a short walk away, you'll find *The Haunted Mansion*, a spooky yet fun attraction that's perfect for fans of the supernatural. Step inside the creepy, old mansion, and you'll be greeted by a ghostly host who introduces you to the 999 "happy haunts" who live there. As you board your "doom buggy," the mansion comes to life with eerie sounds, floating ghosts, and rooms that seem to stretch and change before your eyes. The ride blends scares and laughs perfectly, making it feel like a haunted house with a playful twist. The Haunted Mansion is famous for its special effects, from the dancing ghosts in the ballroom to the invisible instruments playing spooky music. And during Halloween and Christmas, the mansion gets a special holiday makeover inspired by *The Nightmare Before Christmas*, adding a unique twist to the spooky fun.

For those looking for a big thrill, *Space Mountain* in Tomorrowland is a must-do. This indoor roller coaster takes you on a high-speed journey through outer space, with twists, turns, and drops that keep you on the edge of your seat. In the dark, all you can see are twinkling stars and galaxies, making it feel like you're really rocketing through space. The futuristic music and special effects add to the experience, making it one of the most thrilling rides in the park. Space Mountain is perfect for adventurers who love the thrill of the unknown, and it's one of those rides you'll want to go on again and again. And if you're visiting during certain times of the year, you might get to experience a special version of the ride, like *Hyperspace Mountain*, which adds a Star Wars theme to the journey, complete with music and sound effects from the galaxy far, far away.

For a taste of the Old West, *Big Thunder Mountain Railroad* in Frontierland is an absolute must. Known as "the wildest ride in the wilderness," this roller coaster takes you through an abandoned gold mine filled with sharp turns, drops, and surprises. The setting is filled with animatronic animals, crumbling rock structures, and even an explosive finale that adds to the excitement. The ride speeds up and slows down at unexpected moments, making it feel like your mine train is out of control. As you twist and turn through the mountain, you'll see scenes of the Old West, complete with mining equipment and mountain goats standing on rocky ledges. It's a fun mix of excitement and charm, and the beautiful desert scenery around the mountain makes it feel like you're really out in the wilderness.

No visit to Disneyland would be complete without riding *It's a Small World*, a boat ride that takes you on a colorful journey around the world. This classic attraction is famous for its cheerful song and the many dolls representing different cultures, all singing together in harmony. As your boat floats along, you'll pass through scenes filled with characters, animals, and landmarks from places like Africa, Asia, Europe, and South America. The ride is colorful and cheerful, with a message of unity and peace that makes it special for visitors of all ages. Kids love spotting the different animals and costumes, and the catchy tune is one you'll find yourself humming long after the ride is over. Plus, the outside of the ride, with its beautiful white and gold facade, is one of the most iconic spots in the park.

For younger kids or anyone who loves gentle rides with a touch of magic, *Peter Pan's Flight* in Fantasyland is a must-ride. This enchanting attraction lets you board a flying pirate ship and soar over scenes from *Peter Pan*, including the rooftops of London and the magical island of Neverland. As you "fly" through the ride, you'll see Captain Hook, Tinker Bell, and other beloved characters from the story, all brought to life with vibrant colors and whimsical details. The ride feels like a trip straight into a storybook, and the gentle motion makes it perfect for kids and adults alike. It's a favorite among Disneyland visitors, and the feeling of flying over the twinkling city lights of London is pure magic.

For fans of high-speed thrills, *Indiana Jones Adventure* in Adventureland is a must-do. This intense, action-packed ride takes you on a journey deep into a mysterious temple, where you encounter traps, rolling boulders, and creepy creatures. You board a rugged jeep that bounces and races through dark passageways, dodging dangerous obstacles along the way. With special effects that make you feel like you're right in the middle of an Indiana Jones movie, this ride is thrilling from start to finish. The attention to detail is incredible, from the ancient carvings on the temple walls to the eerie sounds echoing through the darkness. Every twist and turn of the ride feels unpredictable, adding to the sense of adventure. It's perfect for anyone who loves a thrill and a taste of danger.

Splash Mountain in Critter Country is another iconic Disneyland ride that combines fun storytelling with a splashy ending. This log flume ride tells the story of Br'er Rabbit's journey to find his "laughing place," with scenes featuring Br'er Fox, Br'er Bear, and other animal friends. The ride takes you through peaceful, scenic sections, with songs like "Zip-a-Dee-Doo-Dah" playing in the background, but it also has exciting drops and twists. The grand finale is a huge plunge down a waterfall, where you're sure to get soaked! The mix of music, scenery, and thrill makes Splash Mountain a perfect family ride, and on a hot day, it's a refreshing way to cool off.

In Star Wars: Galaxy's Edge, *Millennium Falcon: Smugglers Run* is a must-do for any Star Wars fan. This interactive ride lets you step inside the iconic Millennium Falcon and take on the role of pilot, gunner, or engineer as you go on a mission through the galaxy. The cockpit is filled with buttons, levers, and screens that make you feel like a real space traveler. Depending on your role, you'll be asked to complete tasks to help navigate or defend the ship, and the outcome of the mission depends on how well the team works together. It's a one-of-a-kind experience that puts you right in the middle of a Star Wars adventure, and the thrill of flying the Millennium Falcon is unforgettable.

Another must-do in Galaxy's Edge is *Star Wars: Rise of the Resistance*, an epic attraction that combines multiple ride types to create a completely immersive experience. In this attraction, you join the Resistance in a battle against the First Order, with appearances by characters like Rey, Kylo Ren, and BB-8. The ride includes thrilling sequences, from a face-off with Stormtroopers to an escape in a Resistance shuttle, all with mind-blowing effects that make you feel like you're truly in a galaxy far, far away. Rise of the Resistance is one of the most popular rides in Disneyland, and it's known for its amazing storytelling and groundbreaking technology.

Disneyland's *Matterhorn Bobsleds* is a must-do for fans of classic roller coasters. This unique coaster takes you up and down a snow-capped mountain, with twists, turns, and drops that make it feel like a bobsled race. As you speed through the mountain, you'll encounter the mysterious Yeti, who lurks in the icy caves, adding a touch of suspense to the adventure. The Matterhorn was Disneyland's first roller coaster and remains a fan favorite for its thrilling track and beautiful mountain scenery.

Each of these rides brings something different, from the high-speed thrills of roller coasters and space adventures to the gentle magic of Fantasyland. Whether it's your first visit or your hundredth, these must-do attractions capture the wonder and excitement that make Disneyland a place like no other. With each ride offering its own unique story, every part of your day will feel like a new chapter in a fantastic adventure.

Chapter 11: Meet the Characters and Take a Selfie

Meeting Disney characters in Disneyland is one of the most magical parts of any visit, and for kids, it's like getting to step into a storybook where their favorite characters come to life! Disneyland is filled with beloved characters ready to meet guests, pose for pictures, and create unforgettable memories. From classic characters like Mickey Mouse and Minnie Mouse to newer favorites like Moana and Elsa, every corner of the park offers a chance to make friends with the stars of Disney's most famous movies. Whether you're exploring Fantasyland, wandering around Adventureland, or venturing into Tomorrowland, there's always the possibility of a magical encounter.

Mickey Mouse, the character that started it all, is often seen in places like Main Street, U.S.A. or Mickey's Toontown. Getting to meet Mickey is a huge highlight for many visitors, and he's usually dressed in his classic red shorts, yellow shoes, and white gloves, looking just like he does in the cartoons. Meeting Mickey in person feels like meeting a real celebrity! Mickey loves to pose with his friends, and he's always ready with a wave, a hug, or a cheerful "Oh boy!" You might even meet him in different outfits, depending on the season or event. For example, during Halloween, Mickey wears a costume, and during Christmas, he's often seen in festive holiday attire. Every encounter with Mickey feels special, and it's always a treat to take a selfie with him and capture the moment forever.

Close by, Minnie Mouse is often spotted looking stylish in her signature polka-dot dress and bow. Minnie is super sweet, and she's always excited to meet her fans, especially those who show up wearing their own Minnie ears! Her gentle, friendly personality makes her a favorite for little ones, and she loves to pose and even blow a kiss or two for the camera. Minnie's outfits also change for special occasions—during holidays, she sometimes wears a winter coat, and on other days, you might see her in a fun floral dress. A photo with Minnie is a must for any Disney fan, and she's often found near her house in Toontown, making it feel like you're stepping right into her world.

Over in Fantasyland, the Disney princesses are waiting to meet guests in their royal finery. Princesses like Cinderella, Snow White, Belle, Ariel, and Rapunzel are often seen near the Royal Hall or the Fantasy Faire area. Meeting a princess is like entering a fairytale—each princess has her own unique story, and they love to chat with guests about their adventures. Cinderella might ask if you've seen her glass slipper, while Ariel loves to talk about her underwater friends. The princesses are always excited to share stories, answer questions, and take photos. Each princess looks just as she does in the movies, with sparkling gowns, jewels, and crowns that make them feel like real royalty. Taking a selfie with a princess is like capturing a fairytale moment to keep forever!

Over in Adventureland, you can often find characters like Aladdin, Jasmine, and even Genie, ready to welcome guests to the exotic and exciting world of Agrabah. Aladdin and Jasmine are playful and love talking about their adventures on the magic carpet, and Genie is always full of jokes and laughs. Adventureland is also where you might see Moana, who's always excited to talk about her ocean voyages and her love for the island of Motunui. Moana is fun, friendly, and loves to talk to guests about the ocean and the importance of following your heart. Meeting her feels like stepping into the world of the Pacific islands, and she's more than happy to pose for a selfie with a big, warm smile.

In Frontierland, Woody and Jessie from *Toy Story* are ready to welcome you to the Wild West! Woody, in his cowboy hat and sheriff's badge, is always up for an adventure, and Jessie, with her bright red hat and friendly attitude, is just as fun and lively. They love meeting young cowboys and cowgirls and often give high-fives, hugs, and funny poses for photos. Woody and Jessie's playful personalities make every encounter feel like you're right in the world of *Toy Story*, and they're always thrilled to take selfies with their fans. Sometimes, Buzz Lightyear even makes an appearance nearby in Tomorrowland, where he'll salute guests with a cheerful "To infinity and beyond!" Buzz loves striking heroic poses, and taking a photo with him feels like you're teaming up for a galactic adventure.

In New Orleans Square, Jack Skellington and Sally from *The Nightmare Before Christmas* sometimes appear, especially around Halloween and Christmas. Jack is tall, slim, and very friendly, with his black pinstripe suit and iconic skull face, while Sally is soft-spoken and sweet, with her patchwork dress and long red hair. Meeting Jack and Sally feels like stepping into Halloween Town, and they're always eager to chat about spooky fun and the importance of being yourself. Jack loves posing with his bony hand resting on his chin or holding out his hand dramatically, making for an unforgettable selfie. Sally, with her thoughtful and gentle personality, adds a touch of mystery and magic to the experience, and together they create a Halloween moment you'll never forget.

In Galaxy's Edge, Star Wars fans can meet characters from a galaxy far, far away. Rey, the brave Jedi, is often seen in the Resistance area, talking to guests about her fight against the First Order and her mission to protect the galaxy. She's inspiring and full of energy, always ready to chat with young Jedi-in-training or pose for a determined, heroic photo. Chewbacca, the beloved Wookiee, can also be found in Galaxy's Edge. He's incredibly friendly, and even though he doesn't speak English, he's great at communicating with his big, warm hugs and joyful roars. Meeting Chewbacca is an unforgettable experience—he's tall, fuzzy, and incredibly gentle, and a selfie with him is a keepsake for any Star Wars fan.

Of course, Darth Vader and Kylo Ren sometimes make appearances too, bringing a bit of the Dark Side into the park. With their intense expressions and intimidating presence, both characters are popular with fans who love the thrill of meeting a powerful villain. Kylo Ren often appears in front of his ship, and he takes his character seriously—don't expect a smile, but his stern poses and dramatic gestures make for an awesome photo op. Darth Vader, with his iconic black helmet and heavy breathing, is equally impressive, and even though he's a villain, he's a favorite character to take photos with. Standing next to Darth Vader feels like being part of the Star Wars universe, adding an epic touch to any selfie.

And for younger fans, meeting characters like Winnie the Pooh, Tigger, and Eeyore in Critter Country is a must-do. Pooh is gentle and friendly, and he loves big bear hugs, while Tigger is always bouncing and full of energy, making every meeting feel like a little adventure in the Hundred Acre Wood. Eeyore, with his shy but lovable personality, might not smile much, but he's always willing to pose for a photo. Each character is incredibly huggable and ready to make kids feel like they're part of Pooh's world.

Throughout the park, you can also find Disney's newest heroes, like Elsa and Anna from *Frozen*, who sometimes appear in Fantasyland or during special events. Elsa, with her sparkling ice-blue dress and snowy powers, is graceful and warm, while Anna is bubbly and excited to talk about her sister and the kingdom of Arendelle. The two sisters love meeting young fans, and a photo with Elsa or Anna feels like a scene straight from the movie.

Disneyland makes meeting characters even easier by offering the Disneyland app, which shows you where and when characters will appear around the park. This way, you can plan your day and make sure you don't miss anyone on your list. There are also character dining experiences, where you can meet characters while enjoying a meal. These dining spots, like the Plaza Inn, offer a chance to interact with Mickey, Minnie, and other favorites in a cozy setting where they come to each table for photos, autographs, and laughs.

Taking a selfie with a Disney character is more than just a photo—it's a memory that you'll treasure. Every character encounter at Disneyland is filled with magic, from the costumes and voices to the friendly way each character interacts with guests. So, bring your camera, practice your best poses, and get ready to make some amazing memories with the characters you love. Each selfie is like a little piece of Disney magic that you can keep with you, reminding you of the fun and wonder of your day at the happiest place on Earth.

Chapter 12: The Magic Behind Disneyland Rides

The magic behind Disneyland rides is something truly special, filled with creativity, technology, and storytelling that make each attraction feel like its own little world. Every ride at Disneyland is carefully designed to make you feel like you've stepped into a different time or place, whether it's a haunted mansion, an ancient temple, or a galaxy far, far away. Imagineers, the brilliant minds behind Disney attractions, blend art and engineering to create experiences that feel both realistic and magical. They pay close attention to every detail, from the way a ride moves to the sounds, smells, and even the temperature, creating an atmosphere that pulls you right into the story. Disney Imagineers use special effects, animatronics, lighting, and sounds to make every part of the ride come to life, creating a sense of wonder and adventure that you can't find anywhere else.

One of the first things Imagineers think about when designing a ride is the theme. They want every attraction to tell a story, so they start with an idea, like pirates or outer space, and then build everything around that theme. For example, *Pirates of the Caribbean* is themed to make you feel like you're part of a pirate adventure. The designers worked hard to create scenes that look like real pirate towns, with wooden buildings, barrels of treasure, and even skeletons of long-lost pirates. They added the smell of seawater and the sound of waves to make it feel like you're sailing through the Caribbean. Every small detail helps to make the story feel real, so as soon as you step on the boat, you feel like you're part of the pirate world.

Another amazing aspect of Disney rides is the use of animatronics. Animatronics are lifelike robots that can move, talk, and act just like real characters. These animatronics are used in rides like *The Haunted Mansion*, *It's a Small World*, and *Pirates of the Caribbean*, where they play the roles of ghosts, dolls, pirates, and other characters. In *Pirates of the Caribbean*, for example, the pirates look so real because of the way they move and interact with the environment. Some are playing instruments, some are fighting, and others are singing, making it feel like you're surrounded by real pirates. Imagineers spend a lot of time designing these animatronics to move in realistic ways, so they create special motors and programming to make each character move smoothly and naturally. Each animatronic character adds life to the ride, making it feel like you're really in the middle of the story.

One of the most advanced rides, *Star Wars: Rise of the Resistance*, shows how far Disney has come in using technology to create magic. This ride combines animatronics, screen effects, and even trackless vehicles to make it feel like you're truly in a Star Wars adventure. Instead of just sitting in one vehicle for the whole ride, guests move between different parts, each one revealing a new part of the story. You might be escaping from a First Order Star Destroyer one minute, and the next, you're face-to-face with Kylo Ren! The trackless vehicles allow the ride to be unpredictable, so each time you go on it, you might notice something new. It's a completely immersive experience, with sound effects, flashing lights, and even blaster fire that feels so real. This ride pushes the boundaries of theme park technology and shows how Disney is always looking for new ways to surprise and amaze guests.

In *The Haunted Mansion*, Imagineers use a technique called "Pepper's Ghost" to make the ghostly figures in the ballroom appear and disappear like magic. This effect uses reflections and lighting to create an illusion that looks like real ghosts are floating through the room, dancing and celebrating right in front of you. The effect has been used for over a hundred years, but Disney takes it to a new level by using it with moving animatronics, creating an illusion that feels both spooky and real. You'll see ghosts waltzing, playing musical instruments, and even popping up to give you a fright, all thanks to this special effect.

Disneyland rides also use sound to help tell the story. Each attraction has its own soundtrack, often created by famous composers, that fits perfectly with the ride's theme. For example, in *Space Mountain*, the music makes you feel like you're zooming through outer space. The sounds of rushing wind, beeping control panels, and a fast-paced soundtrack add to the excitement, making it feel like you're on an actual space mission. In *Indiana Jones Adventure*, you hear the sounds of crumbling rocks, creepy crawlers, and ancient drums that make it feel like you're in a dangerous temple. Imagineers carefully design the sounds for each scene to make them as immersive as possible, using speakers hidden in walls, floors, and seats so the sounds seem to come from all around you.

Lighting is another important part of Disneyland's magic. Imagineers use lights to change the mood and make the scenes feel more dramatic. In *Big Thunder Mountain Railroad*, for example, flickering lights make it look like the old mining equipment is still running, and in *Matterhorn Bobsleds*, dim lighting and fog effects make it feel like you're on a snowy mountain. In *The Haunted Mansion*, eerie blue and green lighting make the ghostly figures look even spookier, casting shadows and making the scenes feel mysterious and supernatural. Imagineers even change the colors of the lights depending on the season or time of day, so some rides look different at night than they do in the daytime, adding to the magic of the park.

One of the biggest secrets behind Disneyland's rides is the use of special smells, known as "scent effects." These scents help make each ride feel more real by adding another layer to the experience. For example, on *Pirates of the Caribbean*, you might notice the smell of salty sea air, as if you're actually on the ocean. In *Soarin' Over California*, guests can smell the scent of oranges as they fly over California's orange groves and the fresh pine smell as they soar over forests. These scents are pumped into the air at just the right time, so they match the scenes and make you feel like you're really there. Disney uses these smells in many rides to make each one feel unique, and guests love spotting them as they go through the attractions.

Projection mapping is another magical tool that Disney uses to bring stories to life. In *Radiator Springs Racers*, projection mapping is used to show the characters' faces as they talk and interact, making the cars look like they're alive. In *Peter Pan's Flight*, projections are used to make the city of London sparkle below you as you fly over it, giving the illusion that you're really soaring through the sky. By projecting images onto different surfaces, Imagineers can create effects that look almost like moving paintings, blending them with the physical sets to make the whole scene come to life. This technique adds a magical layer to rides, creating moments that seem to defy reality.

And, of course, Disneyland uses cutting-edge ride technology to make everything run smoothly and feel more exciting. From the classic dark rides with their gentle tracks to the high-speed coasters, Disney designs each ride system to match the story it's telling. In *The Haunted Mansion*, the "doom buggies" move smoothly through each scene, turning to show you just the right angle, while *Indiana Jones Adventure* uses a motion simulator to make it feel like you're speeding, bouncing, and dodging danger. *Big Thunder Mountain Railroad* uses a train-style roller coaster that speeds up and slows down, giving you the feeling of a runaway train in the Wild West. Each type of ride system is chosen to create a specific feeling, whether it's a gentle drift through *It's a Small World* or the stomach-dropping thrills of *Guardians of the Galaxy – Mission: Breakout!*.

Even outside the rides, Imagineers add hidden secrets to make Disneyland even more magical. You might notice tiny details, like hidden Mickey shapes in the decorations, small carvings, or even secret sounds. In *Indiana Jones Adventure*, there are symbols on the walls that you can translate using special cards, and in *The Haunted Mansion*, you might spot a "ring" embedded in the ground as part of the story. These little Easter eggs, as they're called, are placed all around the park for guests to discover, making Disneyland feel like a world full of hidden magic.

All these different elements come together to create the magic behind Disneyland rides. Each attraction combines story, technology, and design to make the experience feel completely immersive, whether you're flying over Neverland, exploring a pirate cove, or escaping from a haunted mansion. Every sound, light, smell, and animatronic adds to the feeling that you're part of an adventure, creating moments that stay with you long after you've left the park. This attention to detail and commitment to magic is what makes Disneyland rides unlike any other.

Chapter 13: Disneyland's Most Delicious Treats

Disneyland is known for more than just its rides and shows—it's also home to some of the tastiest, most creative treats you'll find anywhere! Disneyland's food is part of the magical experience, with snacks and desserts that look and taste amazing. Each area of the park has its own unique treats, and some of them have even become famous among fans. Whether you're in the mood for something sweet, salty, or fruity, there's always a delicious snack waiting for you around the corner. From churros and Dole Whip to Mickey-shaped pretzels, every treat is packed with flavor and Disney magic.

One of the most popular treats in Disneyland is the classic churro. Churros are long, golden sticks of fried dough that are crispy on the outside and soft on the inside, rolled in cinnamon sugar for an extra-sweet kick. You can find churro carts all over the park, and each one has fresh, warm churros that are perfect for munching on as you explore. They're an easy-to-carry snack, so you can eat them while waiting in line for a ride or watching a parade. Disneyland even offers seasonal churro flavors, like pumpkin spice in the fall, peppermint during the holidays, and fruity ones in the summer. These churros add a special twist to the classic snack, and they're always a hit with fans who can't wait to see what new flavor will pop up next.

Dole Whip is another iconic Disneyland treat, especially for fans of all things fruity and refreshing. This creamy, soft-serve pineapple dessert is like a tropical paradise in a cup, and it's served at the Tiki Juice Bar in Adventureland, right by the Enchanted Tiki Room. On a hot day, a cup of cold, sweet Dole Whip is the perfect way to cool down. You can also get it as a Dole Whip float, with pineapple juice poured over the top, making it extra fruity and refreshing. Dole Whip has become so popular that it's now considered one of Disneyland's "must-try" treats. The smooth, tangy flavor is like a mini tropical vacation in every bite, and it's especially great for fans who want a lighter dessert option that's still packed with flavor.

When it comes to sweet treats, Disneyland's churros and Dole Whip are just the beginning. Mickey-shaped treats are a huge favorite at Disneyland, and they come in so many forms! Mickey pretzels are a classic choice—they're soft, warm, and shaped just like Mickey's head, making them a fun and delicious snack. You can find Mickey pretzels at various carts around the park, and they're usually served with a side of cheese sauce for dipping. The combination of salty pretzel and creamy cheese makes for a savory snack that's perfect for taking a break between rides.

Another fan favorite is the Mickey-shaped ice cream bar. This treat features creamy vanilla ice cream coated in a thick layer of chocolate, all shaped like Mickey's head. It's a simple but delicious dessert that's perfect for a hot day, and it's easy to eat while you walk around the park. Taking a bite out of a Mickey ice cream bar feels like a classic Disneyland experience, and it's one of those treats that people love to snap a photo of before digging in. There's also a Mickey-shaped cookie option, which is large, chocolate-dipped, and perfect for sharing—or enjoying all by yourself!

In New Orleans Square, you'll find a treat that's as delicious as it is unique: the beignet. Beignets are fluffy, square-shaped donuts covered in powdered sugar, and they're served hot, so each bite is warm and sweet. You can get these tasty treats at the Mint Julep Bar, which is also known for its refreshing mint julep drinks. The combination of a sugary beignet with a cool mint julep is a perfect pairing, and it's a favorite stop for fans who want to experience a taste of New Orleans. Disneyland sometimes offers seasonal beignet flavors too, like pumpkin spice or peppermint, adding a festive twist to this classic snack. Beignets are a little messy (thanks to all that powdered sugar!), but that's part of the fun. You'll see lots of people walking around with powdered sugar on their clothes after a stop at the Mint Julep Bar.

For chocolate lovers, the Disneyland Resort has plenty of options, but one of the best is the churro toffee. This unique treat can be found at Marceline's Confectionery in Downtown Disney or at Candy Palace on Main Street, U.S.A. Churro toffee is made with buttery toffee coated in white chocolate and then sprinkled with cinnamon sugar, giving it a flavor similar to a churro but with a delightful crunch. The combination of sweet white chocolate, crunchy toffee, and cinnamon sugar makes it a popular choice for fans with a sweet tooth. It's also a great treat to bring home, as it's wrapped and ready to take as a souvenir or a gift for friends and family.

In Frontierland, hungry guests can head over to the Golden Horseshoe for a refreshing treat called the ice cream float. This dessert is made with a generous scoop of vanilla ice cream dropped into a cup of fizzy soda, creating a creamy, bubbly treat that's both refreshing and satisfying. Root beer is a popular choice for the float, but sometimes they offer other flavors like orange or cola. The ice cream float is perfect for cooling off on a warm day, and it's a treat that many families love to share.

Disneyland is also famous for its caramel apples, which you can find at the Candy Palace on Main Street, U.S.A., or at other sweet shops around the park. These aren't your ordinary caramel apples; Disneyland's caramel apples are dipped in rich caramel and then coated in all kinds of delicious toppings. Some are decorated to look like characters, with Mickey and Minnie apples featuring little ears and bows made out of chocolate. Others are covered in nuts, chocolate drizzle, or even candy pieces. These apples are a fun treat to eat because you can slice them into pieces to share, and the combination of sweet caramel and crisp apple is hard to beat. Disneyland often offers special caramel apple designs for holidays, making them an exciting seasonal treat to look out for.

If you're a fan of savory snacks, Disneyland has you covered too. Over in Adventureland, you can find the famous Bengal Barbecue, where they serve skewers of grilled meats and vegetables. The Bengal Barbecue is known for its spicy, flavorful sauces and fresh ingredients, making it a great spot for a quick and tasty snack. There's a variety of skewer options, from chicken to beef to vegetables, so there's something for everyone. This snack is especially popular with people who want something more filling than a churro but still easy to eat on the go.

For a unique, Instagram-worthy treat, check out the galaxy-themed snacks at Star Wars: Galaxy's Edge. Blue and green milk are fan-favorites here, inspired by the drinks seen in the Star Wars movies. These milks aren't actually dairy—they're plant-based and have a slushy-like texture, with flavors that are sweet and fruity. The blue milk has hints of berry flavor, while the green milk has a tropical taste. They're a fun and refreshing drink option that feels straight out of a galaxy far, far away. You'll often see fans taking pictures with their blue or green milk in front of the Millennium Falcon or other Star Wars landmarks in Galaxy's Edge, making it one of the trendiest treats in the park.

Finally, at Disneyland's Plaza Inn, you can enjoy one of the most famous meals in the park: fried chicken. This meal features crispy, golden fried chicken served with mashed potatoes, vegetables, and a fluffy biscuit. It's a hearty, delicious meal that's perfect for when you need a break from walking and want to sit down and enjoy a classic comfort food. The fried chicken at Plaza Inn is so popular that it's become a must-try for many visitors, and it's great for families who want to share a big, satisfying meal together.

From sweet to savory, frozen to fried, Disneyland's treats are as magical as the rides and shows. Each snack is crafted with creativity and a touch of Disney magic, turning simple ingredients into unforgettable treats that make your Disneyland visit even more special. The variety of flavors, shapes, and designs make Disneyland's snacks an adventure all on their own, so be sure to try as many as you can. You might even discover a new favorite treat that makes your Disneyland memories even sweeter!

Chapter 14: Parades and Shows You Can't Miss

Parades and shows are a huge part of what makes Disneyland so magical. These events bring together characters, music, dancing, and even fireworks to create special moments that you can only experience in the park. From colorful daytime parades filled with beloved Disney characters to incredible nighttime shows that light up the sky, Disneyland's entertainment is just as enchanting as the rides. Each parade and show has its own theme and story, drawing you into Disney worlds and making you feel like you're part of the adventure. They're so popular that people line up early just to get a good spot to watch, and it's easy to see why—they're full of surprises, magic, and the joy of seeing Disney characters come to life.

One of the biggest and most beloved parades at Disneyland is the *Magic Happens* parade. This parade is a celebration of Disney's storytelling magic and brings together characters from classics like *Sleeping Beauty* and *The Little Mermaid* as well as newer favorites like *Frozen 2* and *Moana*. Each float is beautifully designed to match the theme of the movie it represents. For example, Moana rides on a wave-shaped float, gliding through the parade route as if she's actually on the ocean. Elsa, from *Frozen 2*, has a float that sparkles with icy blue and white colors, making it look like she's summoning snow and ice magic right there in front of you. The music in *Magic Happens* is upbeat and catchy, and each float's design and decorations are crafted with incredible detail, so you feel like you're walking through the scenes of your favorite Disney movies. This parade also includes dancers dressed in costumes that match each float's theme, adding extra flair and movement to the parade. When you watch *Magic Happens*, you feel like you're part of the Disney magic, and it's an experience that makes fans of all ages smile.

Another unforgettable experience is the *Fantasmic!* nighttime show. This show takes place on the Rivers of America, where lights, water, fire, and music come together to tell the story of Mickey Mouse battling villains and celebrating dreams. *Fantasmic!* is one of Disneyland's most spectacular shows because it combines so many different elements. Mickey starts the show by appearing in his sorcerer's hat and cape, casting magical spells as fountains of water shoot up around him. As the show unfolds, scenes from Disney movies like *Aladdin*, *The Lion King*, and *Pocahontas* are projected onto giant water screens, creating a colorful, dreamlike effect. One of the most exciting parts of *Fantasmic!* is when a huge, fire-breathing dragon (representing Maleficent from *Sleeping Beauty*) appears and battles Mickey, adding a thrilling, larger-than-life moment. With the mix of live characters, dazzling effects, and classic Disney music, *Fantasmic!* is a show that feels like stepping into Mickey's dreams. The entire show feels magical and keeps you on the edge of your seat, especially when fireworks light up the sky at the end, adding a breathtaking finish to the experience.

If you love fireworks, the *Disneyland Forever* fireworks show is something you absolutely can't miss. This nighttime show is not just about the fireworks but also includes projections that transform Sleeping Beauty Castle, Main Street, U.S.A., and other parts of Disneyland into scenes from beloved Disney films. You'll see moments from *The Lion King*, *Frozen*, *Finding Nemo*, and more displayed across the park as the sky fills with sparkling fireworks. The show's music brings even more magic, with classic Disney songs that match each projection, like "Circle of Life" for *The Lion King* or "Part of Your World" for *The Little Mermaid*. The fireworks are timed perfectly with the music and projections, creating a spectacular effect that makes it feel like the entire park is part of a Disney movie. What makes *Disneyland Forever* extra special is that you can watch it from multiple areas in the park, and each spot offers a unique view. Watching from Main Street, U.S.A. gives you a great view of the castle, while spots near Rivers of America let you see projections on the water. *Disneyland Forever* is a show that fills the entire park with Disney magic, and it's a favorite for both kids and adults.

Another parade that has become a Disneyland legend is the *Main Street Electrical Parade*. This parade has been around for many years, and fans love it for its dazzling lights and catchy music. Every float in this parade is covered in thousands of colorful, twinkling lights, making it a sight to behold, especially when it moves through the park at night. The floats feature characters like Alice in Wonderland, Peter Pan, and the Seven Dwarfs, all glowing with bright colors. One of the most famous floats is the giant, sparkling Elliott, the dragon from *Pete's Dragon*, which seems to "breathe" green smoke as it makes its way along the parade route. The *Main Street Electrical Parade* also features the famous "Baroque Hoedown" music, a cheerful and electronic tune that fans immediately recognize. Watching the lights and hearing the music makes this parade feel almost magical, like a dream come to life. The *Main Street Electrical Parade* is a classic that many Disney fans cherish, and it's a beautiful, nostalgic way to end a day at Disneyland.

The *Mickey and the Magical Map* show is another must-see, located in the Fantasyland Theatre. This stage show combines live performers, animated characters, and a magical map that comes to life. In this show, Mickey Mouse dreams of becoming a mapmaker and gets whisked away on an adventure through different Disney worlds. The magical map guides Mickey through scenes with beloved Disney characters like Pocahontas, Mulan, and King Louie from *The Jungle Book*, who each perform songs from their movies. The map itself is a giant, moving screen that displays stunning animated backgrounds, making it feel like Mickey and the characters are truly traveling through these worlds. With catchy songs, talented dancers, and Mickey's lovable personality, this show is a fun and musical journey for everyone. The theater is shaded, so it's a nice place to relax during a hot day, and the show is perfect for fans who love singing along to Disney songs.

Frozen – Live at the Hyperion is a Broadway-style show located in Disney California Adventure, and it's a treat for anyone who loves the story of *Frozen*. This show retells the story of Anna and Elsa, complete with all the songs from the movie, like "Let It Go" and "Do You Want to Build a Snowman?" The production features beautiful costumes, impressive set designs, and special effects that make it feel like the icy world of Arendelle has come to life. Elsa's magic is recreated with shimmering lights and sounds, making the audience feel like they're watching real ice magic happen on stage. The actors are incredible, bringing the characters to life with amazing performances, and Olaf the snowman even makes an appearance, adding a bit of humor and fun. The show lasts about an hour, making it a great choice for families who want to sit down and enjoy a full-length Disney story with all the music and magic of the movie.

For Star Wars fans, *Star Wars: Galaxy's Edge* has its own form of live entertainment that's a bit different from traditional parades and shows. Throughout the day, you'll see characters like Rey, Kylo Ren, and stormtroopers walking around and interacting with guests. This experience feels more like stepping into the Star Wars universe, as the characters often stay in character and make you feel like you're part of the story. Kylo Ren might approach and question you about the Resistance, while Rey might encourage young fans to join her in the fight against the First Order. There are also mini-shows, like the training sessions where young visitors can learn how to use lightsabers. These interactive experiences make *Star Wars: Galaxy's Edge* feel like a living, breathing world, where guests can experience the magic of Star Wars firsthand.

For a seasonal treat, Disneyland's holiday shows are unforgettable. During Halloween, there's *Halloween Screams*, a nighttime projection and fireworks show featuring Disney villains like Maleficent, Ursula, and Oogie Boogie. The spooky music, green and purple fireworks, and scenes of villains add a thrilling twist to the usual fireworks shows.

During the winter holidays, *Believe... In Holiday Magic* is a special fireworks show that includes Christmas music, festive projections, and even snowfall on Main Street, U.S.A. The holiday shows bring extra joy and excitement to Disneyland, creating a festive atmosphere that makes the park feel like a holiday wonderland.

These parades and shows are a big reason why a trip to Disneyland feels so magical. They bring Disney stories to life in ways that are larger than life, with lights, music, characters, and surprises around every corner. Watching these shows makes you feel like you're part of something truly special, and it's these magical moments that make Disneyland more than just a theme park. They turn a visit into a memorable experience that fans treasure for years to come.

Chapter 15: Fireworks and Nighttime Spectaculars

The fireworks and nighttime spectaculars at Disneyland are some of the most unforgettable experiences in the park. As the sun sets, Disneyland transforms into a world of twinkling lights and enchanting music, where fireworks light up the sky and the magic seems even more real. Fireworks have been a part of Disneyland's history for decades, and each show is carefully designed to match the park's unique spirit. These nighttime spectaculars are more than just a display of colors in the sky—they tell stories, bring Disney characters to life in dazzling ways, and fill the air with melodies from everyone's favorite Disney movies. Whether you're standing in front of Sleeping Beauty Castle, along Main Street, U.S.A., or by the Rivers of America, every view of the fireworks feels magical and special.

One of the most famous fireworks shows is *Disneyland Forever*. This show doesn't just include fireworks but combines them with projections, lighting, and music, making it a full park-wide experience. The show features songs and scenes from Disney classics like *The Lion King*, *Frozen*, *Peter Pan*, *Finding Nemo*, and *The Jungle Book*, all projected onto iconic parts of the park like Sleeping Beauty Castle, Matterhorn, and even the buildings along Main Street, U.S.A. When Simba roars on Pride Rock, or Ariel sings "Part of Your World," the entire park comes alive with colors and music. The fireworks are carefully timed to match the rhythm of the songs, creating a stunning visual effect. Watching from different areas of the park gives you a unique view of the show because each spot has its own special projections and angles. *Disneyland Forever* is a celebration of Disney storytelling, and each part of the show is crafted to make you feel like you're right in the middle of your favorite Disney adventures.

Fantasmic! is another incredible nighttime spectacular that combines fireworks, water fountains, lights, fire, and music to tell the story of Mickey Mouse's dreams and imagination. Taking place on the Rivers of America, *Fantasmic!* is one of Disneyland's most elaborate shows. It begins with Mickey, dressed as the Sorcerer's Apprentice, using his magic to create dancing fountains of water and colorful lights. The show features scenes from Disney classics like *Aladdin*, *The Lion King*, *Beauty and the Beast*, and *The Little Mermaid*, all projected onto huge water screens that make it feel like you're looking into a dream world. One of the most thrilling moments is when Maleficent from *Sleeping Beauty* appears as a giant dragon, breathing real fire as Mickey battles her in a showdown between good and evil. The mix of live actors, animated projections, and special effects makes *Fantasmic!* a show that's hard to look away from. It's packed with exciting scenes, and as Mickey finally defeats the villains and triumphs over the darkness, fireworks explode in the sky, celebrating his victory and filling the night with light and color.

For Star Wars fans, *Star Wars: Galaxy's Edge* offers a nighttime experience that feels like stepping right into the movies. The *Star Wars: A Galactic Spectacular* uses lighting effects, music from the Star Wars films, and even a few fireworks to create the feeling of an epic space battle in the heart of Batuu. While this isn't a traditional fireworks show, the mix of lights, sounds, and projections on the rocky landscape make it feel like the entire area is part of a Star Wars adventure. Seeing the Millennium Falcon lit up at night and hearing the powerful Star Wars theme music gives fans the feeling that they're really in a galaxy far, far away.

During special times of the year, Disneyland creates holiday-themed nighttime spectaculars that make each season even more magical. One of the most popular seasonal shows is *Halloween Screams*, a spooky fireworks and projection show that takes place during Halloween time. Hosted by Jack Skellington from *The*

Nightmare Before Christmas, this show brings Disney villains to life with haunting music, eerie lights, and spooky visuals projected onto Sleeping Beauty Castle and Main Street. Characters like Maleficent, Ursula, and Oogie Boogie make appearances, filling the show with just the right amount of Halloween magic. The music includes classic Halloween songs as well as some of the darker Disney melodies, and green and purple fireworks light up the night in colors that fit the Halloween theme. *Halloween Screams* is a fun, spooky twist on the usual fireworks shows, and it's perfect for fans who love Disney's villains.

During the winter holiday season, Disneyland presents *Believe... In Holiday Magic*, a fireworks show that captures the spirit of Christmas and the joy of the holidays. This show features classic holiday songs like "White Christmas" and "Jingle Bells" mixed with Disney favorites, and the castle is lit up with twinkling lights that look like icicles. Snowflakes are projected onto the buildings along Main Street, making it feel like you're walking through a winter wonderland. One of the highlights of *Believe... In Holiday Magic* is the snowfall that happens at the end of the show. Yes, real snow! Disney uses special machines to create a soft, snowy effect that falls gently on Main Street, U.S.A., and other areas of the park, bringing a true sense of holiday magic. Watching fireworks and snow together is an experience like no other, and it makes *Believe... In Holiday Magic* a favorite for many Disneyland visitors during the holiday season.

The *Mickey's Mix Magic* show is another nighttime spectacular that is perfect for families who love dancing and upbeat music. Instead of traditional Disney songs, *Mickey's Mix Magic* is set to remixed versions of classic Disney tunes, creating a fun, high-energy atmosphere that gets everyone in a party mood. The projections on Sleeping Beauty Castle and Main Street are vibrant and colorful, and they feature Mickey, Minnie, and other Disney characters dancing along to the music. The show has bursts of fireworks on select nights, and even on nights without fireworks, the lively projections and lasers make it feel like a true celebration. *Mickey's Mix Magic* is ideal for kids and families who love dancing along to the beat and want to experience a different kind of Disney magic with lots of lights, colors, and rhythm.

One thing that makes Disneyland's nighttime spectaculars so special is the way they combine so many elements—fireworks, projections, music, and sometimes even water and fire effects. The teams at Disney spend months designing each show to make sure that it captures the essence of Disney magic and gives fans an experience they'll remember for years. Each show is carefully crafted to match the emotions of the music, the themes of the stories, and the beauty of the visuals, creating an experience that touches people's hearts and fills them with wonder. When you watch a Disneyland nighttime spectacular, you're not just seeing a show—you're experiencing a story brought to life in a magical, unforgettable way.

For families who want a special viewing experience, Disneyland offers reserved seating for some of the nighttime spectaculars, including *Fantasmic!* and *Disneyland Forever*. These reserved spots give you the perfect view of the action and allow you to relax and enjoy the show without having to stake out a spot hours in advance. There are also dining packages available for some of the shows, where you can enjoy a meal at a Disneyland restaurant and then receive a voucher for a special viewing area. Watching from these areas can make the experience even more magical, as you get an up-close view of the fireworks, projections, and all the little details that make Disneyland's nighttime shows so special.

Disneyland's fireworks and nighttime spectaculars are more than just entertainment—they're a way of bringing guests together to share in the magic of Disney. These shows are moments where families, friends, and even strangers can stand side by side, all feeling the same excitement, awe, and joy. The sights, sounds, and emotions created during these shows are the kind of memories that last a lifetime, and they're a big part of what makes a visit to Disneyland so memorable. So, when you're at Disneyland, make sure to stay for the fireworks and nighttime shows. They're the perfect way to end a magical day and a beautiful reminder that at Disneyland, dreams really do come true.

Chapter 16: Disneyland's Best Kept Secrets

Disneyland is filled with well-known attractions, dazzling parades, and beloved characters, but some of its most exciting details are hidden away, waiting to be discovered. These "best-kept secrets" are like hidden treasures that most people might overlook. From secret spots to fascinating stories, Disneyland is packed with little surprises that make each visit feel like an adventure, even for guests who have visited many times. These secrets are part of what makes Disneyland so magical, as they reveal unique parts of the park's history, add to the storytelling, and create fun discoveries that add extra magic to your visit.

One of Disneyland's best-kept secrets is the tiny apartment above the Firehouse on Main Street, U.S.A. This apartment belonged to Walt Disney himself, who wanted a place to stay inside the park while it was being built and during its early years. The apartment is small and cozy, with a Victorian-style design that matches the charm of Main Street. Walt would often watch guests from his apartment window, taking in their joy as they experienced Disneyland. To this day, a small lamp in the apartment's window is left on 24/7 as a tribute to Walt, symbolizing that his spirit and vision are always present in Disneyland. When you pass by the Firehouse, you can look up and see the lamp, a quiet reminder of Disneyland's origins and the man who dreamed it all up.

Another hidden treasure is the "secret" basketball court inside the Matterhorn. Although it's not a full-sized basketball court, it's a small area where cast members can shoot some hoops during breaks. This little court is located in the upper part of the Matterhorn mountain, above the track where the bobsled ride operates. In the early days, climbers would scale the outside of the Matterhorn as part of the attraction, and the basketball hoop was installed as a fun activity for them during downtime. Today, the court is still there, and while guests can't visit it, it's a cool secret that not many know about. It's amazing to think that while guests are zooming through the icy caverns on the Matterhorn Bobsleds, there's a hidden spot for shooting hoops just above them!

Have you ever noticed that Disneyland's Haunted Mansion looks like it's sinking? That's because it's actually partially underground! Due to height restrictions in the area and the need for a large indoor space to create the Haunted Mansion's spooky effects, the Imagineers (the team that designs Disney attractions) decided to build part of the ride below ground. After you board the Doom Buggy, you actually go down an elevator, even though it feels like you're just walking into the mansion. This "stretching room" effect not only makes the Haunted Mansion look haunted and mysterious but also cleverly disguises the descent into the ride area. This engineering trick adds to the eerie atmosphere, making it feel like you're being pulled deeper into the mansion's creepy world.

Adventureland has its own set of secrets too, with one of the most fun being the Hidden Mickeys. Hidden Mickeys are small, subtle Mickey Mouse shapes that the Imagineers have placed throughout Disneyland as a kind of "scavenger hunt" for guests. One of the most famous Hidden Mickeys in Adventureland can be found in the Indiana Jones Adventure queue. Look closely at the ropes, gear, and items throughout the queue, and you might just spot a Mickey-shaped design hidden in the details. Hidden Mickeys can be found all over Disneyland, from attraction queues to ride décor and even on some of the food items. Hunting for them can be a fun game, especially if you're looking for something special to do while waiting in line!

The "Secret Club," also known as Club 33, is one of Disneyland's most exclusive spots. Located in New Orleans Square, Club 33 was created as a private club where Walt Disney could entertain special guests and business partners. It's hidden behind an unmarked door, and only a small "33" plaque next to the door gives away its location. Inside, Club 33 has luxurious dining areas decorated in New Orleans-style elegance, and it's filled with Disney memorabilia and artwork that you won't see anywhere else in the park. Membership to Club 33 is very limited, and there's a long waiting list to join. Members and their guests can dine there, making it one of Disneyland's most mysterious and exclusive experiences.

In Tomorrowland, there's a quiet area known as the "Tomorrowland Terrace" where live music performances happen throughout the day. However, this unassuming stage has a magical transformation: it can actually rise up from underground. When it's time for a performance, the stage lifts up with the band already on it, ready to start playing. Back in the 1970s, the Tomorrowland Terrace was known for hosting some of the biggest rock and pop bands, and the stage's ability to "appear" from below added to the futuristic feel of Tomorrowland. Today, it still hosts a variety of musical performances, from classic rock to Disney tunes, and it's a fun surprise to see the stage emerge like magic.

The Main Street windows hold another Disneyland secret, as each one pays tribute to someone important in Disney's history. As you walk down Main Street, take a look at the windows above the shops. Each one features a different name and occupation, but they're not just random—they're tributes to real people who helped make Disneyland and other Disney projects successful. These people might be Imagineers, artists, or Disney executives, and each window has a playful "job title" that reflects their role or personality. For example, one window reads "Royal Decree Publishing Company," honoring the contributions of a Disney scriptwriter. These windows are a clever and heartfelt way to recognize the many people who helped build Disneyland's legacy.

Pirates of the Caribbean has a spooky secret as well. When the ride was first built, Imagineers used real skeletons for some of the props. At the time, they felt that artificial skeletons didn't look realistic enough, so they brought in actual bones from medical schools. Eventually, these real skeletons were replaced with fake ones as technology improved, but it's said that one real skull remains on the ride, hidden among the treasure and pirate skeletons. This detail adds a bit of creepy authenticity to the ride, and it's something fans love to look for as they sail through the dark, eerie caverns filled with treasure and skeletons.

Disneyland also has hidden messages in the ground! If you look closely at the pavement in certain areas, you'll notice some fun designs, especially in places like New Orleans Square and Adventureland. These areas have tiny symbols and designs pressed into the cement that match the theme of each land. For example, in New Orleans Square, you might see fleur-de-lis symbols or tiny leaves in the pavement, which add a touch of New Orleans charm. In Adventureland, you might find tribal patterns or other symbols that match the adventurous, exotic feel of the area. These little touches are easy to overlook but add to the immersive experience, making every step feel like it's part of the story.

There's also a hidden telegraph message in New Orleans Square! At the entrance to the Disneyland Railroad, near the New Orleans Square train station, you can hear the sound of Morse code tapping out a message. This message is actually Walt Disney's opening day speech from when Disneyland first opened in 1955. It's a subtle tribute to Walt and the excitement of Disneyland's opening, hidden in a quiet corner of the park. This tiny detail shows how much thought went into making every part of Disneyland meaningful, down to the smallest sounds.

The Jungle Cruise has some of the funniest hidden secrets of all. The skippers who guide the boats love to make up their own jokes and sometimes even add playful twists to the ride experience. Over the years, the Jungle Cruise has developed a reputation for its silly puns and jokes, with each skipper adding their own style. Some skippers will even share a few "backstage" secrets during the ride, pointing out hidden details in the scenery or making jokes about the animatronic animals. Each skipper has their own personality and jokes, so the Jungle Cruise feels a little different each time you ride it, making it full of surprise and humor that keeps fans coming back for more.

Disneyland's best-kept secrets are a reminder that there's always something new to discover, no matter how many times you've visited. These hidden details, stories, and touches make Disneyland feel like a living, breathing storybook where each corner has a tale to tell. Knowing these secrets adds a new layer of fun to exploring the park, as you can look out for special details, find unexpected surprises, and feel like an insider. Disneyland was built to be a place where imagination comes to life, and these hidden secrets are a big part of what makes it such a magical and timeless destination.

Chapter 17: Animals and Nature at Disneyland

Disneyland isn't just about thrilling rides and amazing characters—there's also a surprising amount of nature and animals hidden throughout the park. From the carefully designed gardens to the real animals that call Disneyland home, the park is a place where people and nature come together in magical ways. Walt Disney himself loved nature, and he wanted Disneyland to be filled with greenery, flowers, and wildlife to make it feel alive. The Imagineers (Disney's designers) worked hard to create an environment that would be lush and welcoming, and they paid attention to even the tiniest details. So, when you walk around Disneyland, you're not just enjoying the attractions—you're also surrounded by carefully planned landscapes, whimsical animal details, and even some real animals that make the experience extra special.

One of the first things you might notice as you step into Disneyland is the abundance of beautiful gardens and plants. Each area of the park has its own theme, and the plants match that theme perfectly. For example, in Adventureland, you'll see palm trees, bamboo, and jungle-like plants that make you feel as though you're deep in a rainforest. In Frontierland, there are cacti, wild grasses, and other plants that fit the feel of the Old West. Even the flowers on Main Street, U.S.A. are carefully chosen to create a welcoming, old-fashioned town square vibe. This thoughtful use of plants and greenery not only adds to the beauty of Disneyland but also helps tell the story of each land, making guests feel like they've stepped into a whole new world.

Disneyland's plants are chosen not just for their beauty but also for how well they fit into each land's theme. In Fantasyland, you might notice soft, colorful flowers that make it feel like you're in a fairytale, while Tomorrowland has more futuristic, space-like plants that look a bit more modern and sleek. The landscaping in Disneyland takes a lot of planning, and the horticulture team (that's the team that takes care of plants) works year-round to keep everything looking fresh and green. They plant seasonal flowers that bloom at different times of the year, so Main Street, U.S.A. always has something new to see, whether it's the bright tulips of spring or the warm-colored chrysanthemums of autumn. Disneyland even has its own greenhouse where they grow plants and experiment with different flowers to see what will look best. This way, they can keep the park looking perfect, no matter the season.

Beyond the beautiful plants, Disneyland has some real animal residents too! One of the most famous Disneyland animals is the group of ducks that live on the Rivers of America and in the various ponds around the park. These ducks have become a charming part of the Disneyland experience, and many guests enjoy spotting them swimming around or waddling along the pathways. The Disneyland ducks have gotten so popular that there are even jokes and stories about them being "official cast members" of the park! These ducks are well-loved, and Disneyland makes sure they're taken care of by providing them with food and safe places to nest. Guests are reminded not to feed the ducks, though, because they have a special diet to keep them healthy.

Another beloved animal feature at Disneyland is the horses on Main Street, U.S.A. These gentle giants pull the Main Street vehicles, like the horse-drawn streetcars, which give visitors a slow, charming ride up and down the street. The horses are well-trained and incredibly friendly, and they've become iconic parts of Disneyland. Disneyland's horses are actually trained at a special facility called the Circle D Ranch, where they're carefully cared for and prepared for their work at the park. These horses are chosen not only for their strength but also for their calm nature, as they work in a busy environment with lots of people around. The horses even get vacations! Every so often, they go back to the ranch to relax, making sure they stay happy and healthy.

Disneyland is also home to a secret population of feral cats! These cats live mostly behind the scenes but can sometimes be spotted in quieter areas of the park. Originally, they were attracted to Disneyland to help control the mice and rat population, and over time, the park has come to embrace them. These cats are actually cared for by Disneyland, which provides them with food and ensures they have places to sleep. Some guests are lucky enough to spot one or two of these cats lounging in a hidden corner, enjoying the sunshine. These furry residents have become a fun part of Disneyland's ecosystem, and while they're not "official" cast members, they do their part to keep Disneyland clean in their own way.

The Jungle Cruise in Adventureland might seem like it's filled with real animals, but most of the animals you see on the ride are actually animatronics. However, the Imagineers did everything they could to make the jungle look as real as possible. The plants around the Jungle Cruise aren't just there for show—they were chosen to create the thick, lush look of a jungle. The area is filled with plants from around the world, including species that can survive in Southern California's climate but look like they belong in the rainforest. As you journey along the river, the dense foliage, hanging vines, and tropical trees make it easy to forget you're in a theme park, and you might even feel like you're on a real jungle expedition.

In addition to the animatronic animals on rides like Jungle Cruise, Disneyland's Rivers of America is home to some actual fish, turtles, and even the occasional visiting bird. The rivers wind around Tom Sawyer Island, and the area is designed to look like a natural, wild river. You'll often see turtles basking on rocks, and sometimes you can spot fish swimming near the surface. Birds like ducks, egrets, and even herons visit the area, adding to the natural feel of Frontierland. Tom Sawyer Island itself has hidden spots where guests can get close to nature, with plenty of shady trees and a quiet atmosphere that makes it a fun place to explore. The island has trails, bridges, and caves that make it feel like a mini wilderness adventure, right in the heart of Disneyland.

Disneyland also has some beautifully designed fountains, ponds, and waterways, which add to the park's natural charm. Sleeping Beauty Castle, for instance, is surrounded by a lovely moat, where ducks and small fish can sometimes be seen swimming. At night, the moat lights up with the castle, creating a magical reflection in the water. The Storybook Land Canal Boats take guests on a gentle ride through scenes from Disney movies, passing by tiny villages, castles, and waterfalls, all with lush gardens and miniatures that look like they belong in a fairytale. This boat ride is a relaxing way to enjoy Disneyland's natural beauty while also exploring some of its magical stories.

Over in Critter Country, nature is the main theme, and this area of the park is designed to look like a peaceful forest. The landscaping is filled with towering trees, wildflowers, and shrubs, creating a cozy atmosphere that feels like a woodland retreat. Critter Country is home to rides like Splash Mountain (soon to be reimagined as *Tiana's Bayou Adventure*), which takes guests through a watery landscape filled with animatronic animals and playful scenes. The landscaping around Splash Mountain is carefully designed to resemble the Southern bayou, with tall reeds, colorful flowers, and swamp-like plants that make the ride feel like it's part of nature. Critter Country also has a few hidden spots where you can sit by the river, listen to the sounds of the forest, and relax in the shade.

Fantasyland has its own natural beauty as well, especially around the Mad Tea Party ride. This area is filled with colorful flowers and whimsical topiaries—bushes trimmed into fun shapes—that give it a fairytale look. The landscaping around Fantasyland is designed to feel magical, with soft greenery and lovely flower beds that look like they could be right out of a storybook. The ponds and streams around

Fantasyland are filled with lily pads and colorful plants, making it feel like a peaceful, enchanted garden.

One special detail in Disneyland is the attention given to butterflies and bees, which help the plants in the park flourish. Disneyland's horticulture team chooses flowers that attract these important pollinators, helping to keep the ecosystem healthy and supporting the park's natural beauty. By planting a variety of flowers and plants, they create a habitat that invites butterflies and bees to visit, adding another layer of life to the gardens. If you keep an eye out, you might spot a butterfly fluttering by or a bee buzzing from flower to flower, quietly helping to make Disneyland even more vibrant.

Disneyland's use of animals and nature extends to its storytelling as well. Each area of the park uses its natural elements to create a mood that fits its story. From the lush, green jungle of Adventureland to the rugged wilderness of Frontierland, the park's plants and natural details are carefully planned to make each land feel real. Disneyland isn't just a place of fantasy—it's a place where nature is honored and used to create an immersive, beautiful world. Even though it's filled with thrilling rides and colorful characters, Disneyland's landscapes and animals give guests a chance to connect with nature, creating a balance between excitement and tranquility.

So, while you're visiting Disneyland, take a moment to look around and appreciate the trees, flowers, animals, and hidden gardens. These natural touches are part of what makes Disneyland so magical, creating a world that's not only filled with fantasy but also connected to the beauty of the real world.

Chapter 18: Souvenir Hunt; Finding Cool Treasures

Going on a souvenir hunt at Disneyland is like a treasure hunt through a world of magic, colors, and surprises! Disneyland is packed with all kinds of keepsakes that help you take a bit of the park's magic home with you. From classic items like Mickey Mouse ears to unique collectibles that can only be found in certain lands, there's something for everyone. The best part about a souvenir hunt is that you never know what treasures you might stumble upon, and every land has something special that reflects its theme. Whether it's a plush character, a shiny pin, or a rare item hidden in a tucked-away store, finding the perfect souvenir adds a fun layer to your Disneyland adventure.

One of the most iconic souvenirs you can find is a pair of Mickey or Minnie ears. These are a must-have for so many visitors and come in a rainbow of styles. Classic black ears with the simple Mickey logo are timeless, but every year Disneyland releases new designs to celebrate special events, new movies, or holidays. There are sparkly ears, themed ears for different characters, and even glow-in-the-dark ears! You can also find customizable Mickey ears with your name embroidered on the back, making it a one-of-a-kind keepsake. Getting a pair of Mickey ears is a fun way to feel like part of the Disneyland family, and the experience of choosing the perfect pair can be a memorable part of your visit.

For those who love to collect small, shiny treasures, pin trading is a Disneyland classic. Disney pins come in hundreds of designs, featuring every character, attraction, and holiday you can think of. Some pins are limited editions, meaning they're only available for a short time, which makes finding them extra exciting. You can trade pins with cast members or other visitors, making the hunt for special pins like a mini adventure. There are pins that represent each land, movie, or even specific attractions, so every time you visit, you can add to your collection. Some people wear their pins on lanyards around their necks, displaying them proudly, while others collect them on boards or in books. Pin trading has become a Disneyland tradition, and you never know what unique designs you might find!

Adventureland offers some of the most exotic souvenirs. Here, you might find Indiana Jones-themed gear, like hats and whips, perfect for aspiring explorers. The Bazaar in Adventureland has treasures inspired by jungles and far-off places, with items like wooden carvings, tiki mugs, and colorful sarongs. If you're a fan of the Jungle Cruise, you can sometimes find themed souvenirs inspired by the ride, such as mini replicas of the boats or vintage-style maps that look like they belong to an explorer. These items make great souvenirs for anyone who dreams of going on wild adventures.

In New Orleans Square, souvenirs have a mysterious charm. Haunted Mansion fans can pick up spooky memorabilia like ghostly figurines, glowing skulls, or even a replica of the iconic "doom buggy" ride vehicle. There are also items featuring the famous "Hitchhiking Ghosts," who are a favorite among Haunted Mansion fans. If you're a fan of the eerie yet fun Pirates of the Caribbean ride, this area is also the best place to find pirate gear! You might find items like pirate swords, eyepatches, hats, and treasure chests, which let you take home a bit of swashbuckling spirit. The shops in New Orleans Square have a magical feel, with items that look like they came from a haunted mansion or a hidden pirate cove, making them extra fun to explore.

Fantasyland is a dreamland for fairytale lovers, and the souvenirs here are straight out of a storybook. You can find wands, tiaras, and princess gowns, allowing young visitors to transform into their favorite Disney royalty. From Snow White to Elsa, there are costumes for nearly every Disney princess. The Bibbidi Bobbidi Boutique is a magical place in Fantasyland where kids can get makeovers and leave looking like royalty. In addition to costumes, Fantasyland is full of toys, figurines, and plush characters from classic Disney movies. There are also souvenirs inspired by rides like Peter Pan's Flight and Alice in Wonderland, including items that have a whimsical feel, like teacup mugs or Mad Hatter hats.

Tomorrowland is the place for futuristic finds. Star Wars fans will be thrilled to explore the Star Wars: Galaxy's Edge area, where they can build their own custom lightsaber at Savi's Workshop or create a personalized droid at the Droid Depot. These are more than just souvenirs—they're interactive experiences where you get to design your own unique piece. The lightsabers are high-quality replicas, complete with glowing blades and sound effects, and each one is different depending on the choices you make during the building process. For those who love Marvel superheroes, Tomorrowland offers action figures, T-shirts, and other hero-themed items, perfect for those who want to take a piece of the Marvel universe home.

One of the most charming Disneyland souvenirs is a pressed penny. Throughout the park, there are machines that let you insert a penny, crank a lever, and press the coin into a unique design. Each machine has a different design, featuring characters, attractions, or Disneyland logos. You can collect these pennies throughout the park, creating a small and affordable collection that captures memories of each ride or land. Some people even buy small books to store their pressed pennies in, keeping them safe as tiny reminders of their Disneyland adventure.

Foodies will love the edible souvenirs Disneyland has to offer. Many people enjoy bringing home treats like Mickey-shaped rice crispy treats, colorful lollipops, or even bags of fresh Disneyland popcorn. These snacks are perfect for sharing the Disneyland magic with friends and family at home or enjoying as a reminder of your visit. Main Street, U.S.A. is filled with candy shops offering fudge, caramel apples, and delicious chocolates, all wrapped in Disneyland's signature packaging. These edible souvenirs can be fun to snack on after you leave the park, bringing back sweet memories with every bite.

The Disneyland hotel gift shops also offer special items that you might not find elsewhere in the park. Here, you can find high-quality clothing, bags, and home decor items that celebrate the Disneyland Resort. There are often unique pieces, like cozy blankets with Mickey designs or stylish Disney-themed home goods, that let you add a touch of Disneyland magic to your everyday life. For a more exclusive souvenir, some visitors check out Disney Gallery, where limited-edition artwork and collectibles can be found. These items are often inspired by Disneyland attractions, characters, or famous Disney scenes and are beautifully crafted, making them perfect for serious Disney fans and collectors.

Then there are seasonal souvenirs, like the holiday-themed items that appear during Halloween and Christmas. During Halloween, Disneyland is filled with spooky merchandise, like pumpkin Mickey ears, Halloween-themed plush toys, and even special Haunted Mansion items. During Christmas, the park offers festive ornaments, cozy holiday sweaters, and limited-edition pins that capture the magic of the season. These seasonal souvenirs are only available for a short time, so they're extra special and make for unique memories.

Lastly, no Disneyland souvenir hunt would be complete without a visit to one of the exclusive Disneyland spirit jersey shops. Spirit jerseys are comfortable, long-sleeve shirts featuring the Disneyland logo on the back, and they come in many colors and designs. Some jerseys glow in the dark, while others are covered in glitter or designed to look like different characters or attractions. These jerseys are incredibly popular and a great way to show your Disneyland pride. You'll often see people wearing them around the park, and they're a cozy reminder of your time at Disneyland long after you've left.

Every corner of Disneyland has its own special souvenirs, making a visit to the park like a treasure hunt with surprises at every turn. Whether you're looking for something small like a pressed penny or something grand like a custom lightsaber, there's a perfect keepsake waiting for you. Disneyland souvenirs are more than just things to take home; they're pieces of the magic you get to keep, reminding you of all the fun, joy, and adventure you experienced at the Happiest Place on Earth.

Chapter 19: Tips for Beating the Long Lines

Navigating Disneyland's long lines is almost like mastering a game, and there are plenty of tricks to help you make the most out of your day without spending too much time waiting. Disneyland is packed with popular rides and attractions, and as fun as they are, they can get pretty crowded, especially during weekends, holidays, and school breaks. But don't worry! With a bit of planning and these handy tips, you can avoid some of the longest lines and enjoy more time having fun. Disneyland experts know all about the best ways to skip, minimize, or totally avoid lines altogether, so here's a full guide to helping you enjoy as many rides and experiences as possible in one magical day.

One of the top secrets to beating long lines is getting to Disneyland early—arriving when the park first opens is called "rope drop." At rope drop, you're among the first people to enter the park, so lines are often shorter, giving you a head start on popular rides. By getting there early, you can hop on a few major attractions before crowds start building up. The best part? Many rides have almost no wait time at rope drop, so you can fit in more rides quickly. If you start with the bigger attractions in the morning, like *Space Mountain*, *Indiana Jones Adventure*, or *Matterhorn Bobsleds*, you can save tons of time, leaving your afternoon free for other experiences, like parades or shows.

Another great tool for beating lines is Disney Genie+, a paid service that lets you reserve times for popular rides, skipping the regular line. With Genie+, you can select a time to return for a ride, and when you get there, you can use the Lightning Lane, which has a much shorter line than the regular standby line. Genie+ is super helpful on busy days and works on many top rides, including *Big Thunder Mountain Railroad*, *Haunted Mansion*, and *Pirates of the Caribbean*. However, it's important to note that you can only book one Genie+

reservation at a time, so it's smart to choose your favorite or busiest rides first, then use your next reservation as soon as you're finished with each one.

For those who love a specific ride and want to make sure they experience it, Individual Lightning Lane is another option. Unlike Genie+, which covers multiple rides, Individual Lightning Lane is available for select, high-demand rides, like *Star Wars: Rise of the Resistance*. By purchasing an Individual Lightning Lane for these rides, you can reserve a specific time to experience them without waiting in the regular line. It's an extra cost, but on extremely busy days, it can save you a lot of time, especially for the park's most popular attractions.

Single Rider lines are a hidden gem for guests who don't mind splitting up from their group to enjoy the ride faster. Some of Disneyland's most popular attractions, like *Matterhorn Bobsleds*, *Indiana Jones Adventure*, and *Millennium Falcon: Smugglers Run*, offer a Single Rider option. When you choose Single Rider, you join a separate, usually much shorter line, and you'll be placed in any available seat by yourself. It's perfect if you're okay with riding solo or if your group doesn't mind splitting up briefly. Single Rider lines can cut down your wait time significantly, so it's worth using for rides with long standby waits.

Timing your ride choices around showtimes and parade times is another smart way to avoid lines. When there's a parade or a show, like the *Main Street Electrical Parade* or *Fantasmic!*, lots of people head to watch, meaning lines for nearby rides often get shorter. If you don't mind skipping a show or parade, that's a great time to enjoy popular rides with less wait time. Many families with younger kids also head to dinner around early evening, so you'll find some lines are shorter during meal hours, typically between 5 and 7 p.m. By riding during these times, you can avoid peak crowds and still have a chance to catch a show later if you plan your time well.

To make the most out of quieter times, try to plan your Disneyland visit on weekdays, especially Tuesdays or Wednesdays, and avoid weekends or holiday periods when possible. The park is generally less crowded on weekdays, especially during the off-season. The off-season times—usually in January and February or September through early November—are when most people are back at school or work, making lines shorter overall. If you can plan a visit during these less busy months, you'll likely spend less time in lines and more time exploring the park.

If you're interested in attractions that offer nighttime experiences, such as *Big Thunder Mountain Railroad* or *Jungle Cruise*, you might want to save these rides for later in the evening. Many people leave the park after the nighttime shows, and some of the lines get shorter as it gets later. Rides like *Big Thunder Mountain* feel entirely different at night, with the desert landscape taking on a spooky glow, and *Jungle Cruise* becomes more mysterious after dark. Plus, later hours mean fewer families with young kids, so you might find shorter wait times.

Disneyland also has entertainment options in line to make waiting more enjoyable. For example, some lines, like those for *Indiana Jones Adventure* and *Star Wars: Millennium Falcon – Smugglers Run*, have interactive elements and themed areas to keep you entertained. *Indiana Jones Adventure* has a detailed queue with artifacts, maps, and secrets that make you feel like you're on a real expedition. *Millennium Falcon's* line includes the famous Falcon ship, Han Solo's gaming table, and plenty of details to explore. Even though you're waiting, it feels like part of the ride experience, helping time pass more quickly.

Another tip is to use the Disneyland app, which is a huge help when it comes to checking ride wait times, managing Genie+ reservations, and even finding food options. The app provides up-to-date information on wait times, which helps you plan your next stop more efficiently. You can even check the wait times from across the park to decide where you want to head next. Plus, with Mobile Order on the app, you can order food and snacks in advance from popular spots like the *Tropical Hideaway* or the *Red Rose Tavern*, skipping the food line and enjoying more ride time.

An often-overlooked way to maximize ride time is to take advantage of attractions with short lines throughout the day. Rides like *The Disneyland Railroad, King Arthur Carrousel, Tarzan's Treehouse,* and *Mark Twain Riverboat* often have shorter lines. These attractions might not be as high-speed or thrilling as the coasters, but they're unique experiences that add a lot to your Disneyland adventure. By visiting these attractions in between bigger rides, you're still having fun without spending too much time in line.

If you're visiting with a group, Rider Switch is another helpful feature, especially for families with younger kids who may not be able to ride every attraction. With Rider Switch, one adult waits with the non-riders while the others enjoy the ride. Then, the waiting adult can ride without going back to the end of the line. It's a great option for parents with little ones, allowing everyone to enjoy the thrill rides without needing to wait twice.

And finally, if you don't mind a few early mornings or late nights, staying at a Disneyland Resort hotel offers "Extra Magic Hour" or "Magic Morning" access, depending on the time of year and your hotel choice. Extra Magic Hour lets you enter Disneyland or Disney California Adventure one hour before the general public on select days. With an extra hour in the morning, you can enjoy several popular rides with little to no wait. This extra hour can make a big difference in your day, giving you a head start on the crowds and letting you fit in more rides early on.

Using a combination of these tips can make a huge difference in your Disneyland experience, helping you avoid long lines, save time, and pack in more rides and activities. Every moment counts at Disneyland, and by planning smartly, you can turn your visit into an even more magical adventure without spending hours waiting in line.

So, whether you're using Genie+, arriving early for rope drop, trying out Single Rider lines, or timing your rides around parades and shows, there are plenty of ways to keep your day moving so you can enjoy as much as possible.

91

Chapter 20: Saying Goodbye; Planning Your Next Trip

As the day winds down and it's time to say goodbye to Disneyland, there's a mixture of emotions—excitement from all the fun you had, and a bit of sadness that the adventure is coming to an end. Saying goodbye to Disneyland isn't easy because there's always so much to do, so much to see, and so much to look forward to on your next visit. But just because it's time to go doesn't mean the magic has to end! Leaving Disneyland gives you a chance to start planning for the next trip, which can be almost as exciting as the visit itself.

Before you officially leave, make sure to take a few final photos in front of some of the park's iconic spots, like Sleeping Beauty Castle, Main Street, U.S.A., or near your favorite ride. Many visitors like to stop by the castle for a goodbye picture because it's such a special and magical spot. Saying goodbye with a final photo helps capture the memories of the day and keeps the magic alive long after you leave. Some families even have a tradition of taking a picture in the same spot every time they visit Disneyland. This way, they can look back and see how they've grown and changed with each visit, keeping a little piece of the Disneyland spirit with them.

As you stroll down Main Street, U.S.A., you might notice that it looks and feels different at the end of the day. The lights on the buildings sparkle as the sky gets darker, creating a warm, nostalgic glow. This part of Disneyland is extra special because it's designed to make you feel like you're stepping back in time, and the evening lights make it feel magical in a new way. Many people like to take a quiet moment to look around and take it all in—the music playing softly, the twinkling lights, and the happy sounds of families sharing their last moments in the park. These final moments are perfect for taking it slow, thinking about your favorite parts of the day, and letting the memories settle in before you leave.

One fun way to wrap up your visit is to check out the gift shops one last time. Disneyland has some special shops on Main Street that stay open a bit later than the rides, so you can do some last-minute shopping before heading out. It's a great time to pick up any souvenirs you may have missed during the day or to grab a sweet treat for the ride home. For many visitors, bringing home a souvenir is like taking a piece of Disneyland with them, whether it's a plush Mickey, a pair of Minnie ears, or a favorite snack like a bag of popcorn or a caramel apple. These items help keep the magic alive at home and remind you of your amazing day. Some people even start collecting Disney souvenirs, adding a new item to their collection each time they visit!

As you leave, you'll likely pass through the exit gates, where you can look back one last time at the magical entrance that welcomed you in the morning. This is a good time to start thinking about all the things you didn't get to do this time, so you can start planning for the future. Disneyland has so many rides, shows, and experiences that it's almost impossible to do it all in one visit. Maybe you missed a ride, didn't get to meet a favorite character, or didn't try a treat you were curious about. But the great thing about Disneyland is that it's always there, ready to welcome you back, and each visit can be a new adventure.

Thinking about your next trip gives you something to look forward to. You might start dreaming about visiting during a different season—Disneyland changes throughout the year with special decorations and events. If you went in the summer, you might want to come back in the fall for Halloween, when the park is filled with pumpkins and spooky decorations. Or, if you visited in spring, maybe you'll plan a winter trip next time, when Disneyland is transformed into a winter wonderland with holiday lights, festive parades, and special seasonal treats. Each season offers new experiences, so no two visits are exactly the same.

If you're a fan of certain characters, you can plan your next trip around meeting more of them. Disneyland has different characters out at different times, and sometimes they're dressed in special outfits to match the season or event. You can also try character dining experiences, where characters come to your table while you eat! By planning your next visit, you can make a list of the characters you didn't get to see and look forward to meeting them next time.

Some families love the idea of creating a Disneyland "bucket list," which is a list of everything they hope to do someday at the park. This could include things like riding every ride, eating at every themed restaurant, or visiting during every holiday season. Making a list helps you remember all the things you want to experience on future trips and keeps the excitement alive as you wait for your next visit. For example, maybe you'll add "try a churro" or "ride Splash Mountain" to your list if you didn't get to do them this time. Disneyland has hidden surprises and unique details in every corner, so there's always something new to discover.

Planning for the next visit also means keeping an eye on any new attractions or changes that might be coming to the park. Disneyland is always updating and adding new experiences, from exciting rides to new lands based on popular movies. If you love Marvel superheroes, you might want to check out Avengers Campus in Disney California Adventure, or if you're a big Star Wars fan, you might want to explore more of Star Wars: Galaxy's Edge. Disney often announces new attractions and shows, so knowing what's coming up can add to the excitement. That way, you're not only looking forward to returning but also to trying something brand new.

Back at home, there are ways to keep the magic alive until your next trip. Watching Disney movies, listening to Disneyland music, or looking at photos from your visit can remind you of all the fun you had. You might even create a scrapbook or photo album with pictures and souvenirs from your trip. Some people make a "Disney jar," where they put money or savings aside little by little to help fund their next adventure. Each time they add to the jar, they're one step closer to another magical day at Disneyland!

If you have friends or family members who have been to Disneyland, talking about your experiences together can be a lot of fun. You can swap stories, share favorite memories, and even give each other tips for future trips. Hearing about other people's adventures can remind you of things you loved and give you new ideas for what to try next time. Disney fans are everywhere, and sharing your memories helps keep the magic alive.

Saying goodbye to Disneyland can feel bittersweet, but with all the memories you've made, you carry a little bit of that magic with you wherever you go. And the best part is, Disneyland is always there, waiting to welcome you back whenever you're ready. Each visit is a chance to create new memories, discover new favorite rides, and explore new lands. The magic of Disneyland doesn't end when you walk out the gates—it stays with you, giving you something wonderful to look forward to until next time. So, until then, keep dreaming about the magic, planning for the fun, and remembering the joy of your visit to the Happiest Place on Earth.

Epilogue

You did it, Disneyland adventurer! You've journeyed through every land, uncovered hidden secrets, and learned all the tips and tricks to make your visit truly magical. Now, you're not just a guest—you're practically a Disneyland expert!

Whether you've just wrapped up an amazing day at the park or are dreaming of your next visit, remember that the magic of Disneyland is always there, waiting for you. Maybe next time, you'll try something new, like a ride you skipped or a food you didn't get to try, or maybe you'll search for a hidden Mickey or a secret spot you missed. The best thing about Disneyland is that there's always something new to discover, no matter how many times you visit.

And even though you're closing this book, keep a little piece of that Disneyland wonder with you. You can be just as brave as a Space Mountain rider, as curious as an explorer in Adventureland, and as joyful as a character in a parade. The magic of Disneyland isn't just in the park—it's also inside *you*.

So, until next time, remember to keep your imagination strong, your spirit adventurous, and your dreams as big as Sleeping Beauty Castle. And who knows? Maybe one day, you'll come back with a whole new set of Disney dreams to make come true.

See you real soon!

The End.

www.ingramcontent.com/pod-product-compliance
Lightning Source LLC
Chambersburg PA
CBHW022033150726
47990CB00002B/936